ALSO BY THE AUTHORS

Baby & Toddler Sleep Solutions for Dummies, Glaser and Lavin. Wiley, 2007 publication date.

Glaser, S. "Parenting" <u>CAJE Early Childhood Publication</u>, Vol 4, June 2006, New York, NY.

Glaser, S. Monthly column in <u>Cleveland On Center</u>, Cleveland OH.

Lavin, A. Chapter 27A - "Newborn Resuscitation" in <u>Common Problems in Obstetric Anesthesia,</u> Datta S. and Ostheimer, W., ed., Year Book Med Publ., 1987, Chicago, IL.

Lavin, A., Nauss, A.H., Newburger, J.W. "A Survey of Pediatric Management of Dyslipidemias in New England." <u>Pediatric Cardiology</u>, 13, 76-79, 1992.

Lavin, A. "Hypothyroidism in Otherwise Healthy Hypercholesterolemic Children." <u>Pediatrics</u>, <u>88 (2)</u>, 332-334, 1991.

Lavin, A., Sung, C., Klibanov, A., and Langer, R. "Enzymatic Removal of Bilirubin from Blood: A Treatment for Neonatal Jaundice." <u>Science: 230</u>, 543-545, 1985.

Who's the Boss?

a parent's guide to raising children and staying sane

moving families from conflict to collaboration

COLLABORATION PRESS

CLEVELAND OH

    Collaboration Press, Inc.
    3733 Park East Drive
    Suite 102
    Beachwood, OH 44122-4334

ORDERING INFORMATION
QUANTITY SALES. Special discounts are available on quantity purchases by corporations, associations, and others. For details, contact the "Special Sales Department" at the address above.

Collaboration Press and their logo are registered trademarks

ISBN 0978789008

LIBRARY OF CONGRESS CONTROL NUMBER 2006931870

SAN 851-6278

PRINTED IN THE UNITED STATES OF AMERICA

FIRST EDITION
10 09 08 07 06 05 04 03 02 01 10 9 8 7 6 5 4 3 2 1

Produced and designed by Randy Martin, martinDESIGN
Cover design by Randy Martin, martinDESIGN, 44118

DEDICATION

This book is dedicated to
Laurel, Rebecca, Joshua, Jeremy, Abigail, and Hannah.

CONTENTS

PREFACE

"WHO'S THE BOSS: MOVING FAMILIES FROM CONFLICT TO COLLABORATION"
was inspired by the privilege of being asked by families to help them
respond to the challenges their children create. Throughout our
many years of practicing pediatrics and directing pre-school pro-
grams, we have been impressed with the emergence of a set of highly
reliable patterns of conflict and challenge between parents and their
young children. Parents frequently face problems in achieving certain goals, such as getting their infant to sleep through the night, or
successfully toilet training their toddler. Parents also frequently feel
challenged by some of their own responsibilities such as feeding their
child or offering appropriate discipline.

We have noted that the advice currently available to parents
tends to be more ideological than practical, and that the ideologies
cluster into two large trends. One ideological trend is to emphasize
the nurturing quality of parenting. This approach asks parents to
solve their issues by offering nothing but love. The other ideology
that dominates the parenting discussions is authority. The advocates
of authority demand that parents impose their will on their children, and it is only in this way that they will grow up to me good,
moral adults.

In both instances, the advice to be more loving and the advice to be
more demanding leave parents with little practical day-to-day guidance on how to solve their most common child-raising dilemmas. In
our many years of working with parents of young children, we have
learned and developed some very practical approaches to managing
the most common problems parents face. Parents with whom we have
shared these ideas have benefitted from these remarkably effective
approaches. In response to parent queries about where they could
find a guide outlining these ideas, we decided it was time to create a
book and make it available to the broader public.

*Who's the Boss: Moving Families from Conflict to Collabora-
tion* offers not an ideology of parenting, but a set of very, very specific approaches to the most common problems parents face in
raising young children. These approaches are very effective. Seeing

what actually works has moved us away from ideology and at the same time has created a philosophy of parenting. Where ideologies impose a strict perspective that cannot bend, adapt, or learn, philosophies offer a stance that invites bending, adapting, and learning.

The philosophy that has emerged, from learning what really helps parents resolve conflicts with children, is that conflicts are a healthy part of childhood and learning.

The ideology of only caring sharply limits parents' ability to offer guidance and shuns conflict. The ideology of authority shares the aversion to conflict but avoids it by making parental guidance unrelated to the child and their perspective.

Our philosophy opens a world of relation between parent and child. We say, respect your child, love your child, learn from your child, guide your child, and together you can manage the inevitable conflicts to very mutual satisfaction.

To all parents and children we offer *Who's the Boss: Moving Families from Conflict to Collaboration* with the hope that you will find mutual respect and real solutions to some of the most vexing problems of early childhood and that these conflicts can come to be viewed as another opportunity to grow closer together.

W

ACKNOWLEDGMENTS

with tremendous gratitude and love, we wish to acknowledge our spouses, Richard Glaser and Diane E. Lavin, without whose support, love, and inspiration this work could not have been done. It was they who helped us reach, explore, learn, and share. Also with gratitude and love, we wish to acknowledge our children. It was they who taught us with their love how to guide and still love.

susan glaser: I wish to thank Jane Kessler, who was my mentor at the Mental Development Center of Case Western Reserve University; Eleanor Weisberger, who inspired me to write a book for parents based on practical, developmentally appropriate ideas that work; my colleagues at the JCC for sharing ideas and strategies; and all the young parents who have entered my life and allowed me to become part of theirs while their families grew and developed.

dr. arthur lavin: No one learns alone. I wish to thank those who most helped me think most broadly about caring for children and their families, how to think carefully about their development, and about the real needs in their lives: Dr. T. Berry Brazelton, Dr. Mel Levine, Dr. F. Sessions Cole, Dr. Phil Hill, Dr. Jerry Hass, and Dr. Alan Nauss. The Division of Community Pediatrics of the American Academy of Pediatrics has filled an important role in my professional development. Dr. F. Edwards Rushton helped create this Division and broadened my concept of what a pediatrician could do to help children. Dr. Cal Sia whose advocacy helped establish the standard that every child deserves a medical home taught me how pediatricians can best advocate for children with special health care needs. The Academy, its staff, and its directors have remained a source of expertise, compassion, and advocacy to help families and their children

finally, we would both like to thank Randy Martin, martinDESIGN, who helped us turn our work into a real book.

W

Introduction

PURPOSE

parenting is one of life's great joys and with it comes some of life's greatest opportunities-and challenges. Many parents feel overwhelmed with the new responsibility of caring for and guiding a young life. Most parents report surprise at the depth and extent of love they immediately feel for their offspring. It is no surprise that this powerful love makes new parents wonder and worry about the *right* way to raise their child.

Parents seem to agree on the fundamental premise that loving and guiding our children is the most extraordinary thing we will ever do. The loving part seems to come naturally, but the guiding part often leaves parents confused and anxious. From the start they are bombarded by conflicting advice from grandparents, friends, magazine articles, and, of course, their own hearts.

It was with the challenge of guiding our children in mind that we wrote this book. Both of us have had the profound privilege of watching how parents have found their own answer to this most important question. We have been granted the opportunity to see which approaches to parenting lead to effective resolution of conflicts, which seem to work well for parents and children, and most importantly, how the inevitable conflicts of childhood can be managed so they result in happy endings.

based on these many decades of experience and listening, we decided to consider the lessons parents have taught us, and present what we have learned to help families think about approaches that work. **Our goal is to make available to you approaches to the most common sources of conflict in parenting young children; approaches that have been proven over and over again to help resolve these conflicts in ways that work. These approaches to resolving conflict enhance both the parents' authority and level of caring, and leave our children feeling more capable, more competent and even more loved.**

We have sought, and developed, approaches that avoid the extremes that we most fear as parents. One is the extreme of *giving in* in which we leave all the decision-making to our infant or toddler in order to avoid conflict. The child, who is not ready to make these decisions, becomes a tyrant and the family is plunged into non-productive interactions which become chronic sources of anxiety and irritation. The other is the extreme of coercion in which we take all the decision-making away from our infant and toddler. In this scenario, children do not learn the important skills of problem solving and the peace of the household is based on a false sense of resolution. Children may comply, but out of fear of punishment, instead of out of a desire to cooperate that will make both them *and* their parents feel satisfied.

Our approaches not only resolve the conflicts of early childhood, they give both parents and children their natural roles in finding the solution. Parents get to offer guidance without compromising their love. Children get to figure out their own solution to the problems that they are largely creating. Together both parents and children enhance their respect for each other, problems are solved, and families get to do more important (and fun!) things than battle.

We hope you find not only detailed answers to some of the most common dilemmas of parenting young children, but also enjoy the wisdom that families have developed in thinking carefully about how best to work together. We think the approaches we present will help you raise your children effectively and in the loving manner you have always dreamed of providing.

HOW TO USE THIS BOOK

the organization of this book is very simple. The first chapter offers a philosophy, the foundation for what follows. Every subsequent chapter is based on this philosophy and offers very detailed, field-tested approaches to solving the most common and vexing challenges of parenting young children.

If you want an overview of how to approach parenting young children, a brief consideration of the history that has created our current sense of challenge is found in   Chapter One. In it you will find a discussion of the concepts of nurturing our children, of the role of conflict on our lives, and of how the goals of loving our kids and teaching our kids have recently varied from long tradition. You will read about how the traditions that once guided parents to balance love and guidance have largely disappeared leaving modern parents challenged to find their own balance. You will read about how today's parents have an historically high commitment today to raising their children in a loving atmosphere and are therefore very worried about how guidance might be misunderstood as being too harsh.

Chapter One, then, takes a careful look at the central challenge of today's young families: how can parents offer guidance without compromising the ultimate goal of being loving and nurturing? We offer our answer to this most central question, and use this philosophy in providing very specific recommendations for how to resolve the most common conflicts that occur in parenting young children.

the rest of the book is a series of chapters orga-
nized by specific challenges. If your need is to solve a pressing problem at hand, feel free to go that chapter. If you are reading this book to specifically end a long conflict around toilet training, go to page 73, Chapter Six and you will have access to a very detailed approach to toilet training that has had a nearly unbroken record of success. Or, if you are exhausted from many months of sleepless nights, responding to your older infants' cries two to three times a night, go to page 17, Chapter Two and you will be treated to another very detailed approach to helping your infant or toddler sleep through the night that also worked very well for essentially every parent that has implemented it.

For sleeping, feeding, toilet-training, disciplining, quieting sibling rivalries, managing child care situations, our book offers answers that we have observed to work time and again for large numbers of families, across large numbers of years. We are excited about making these solutions available to you, and hope you find them more than useful.

We believe that our philosophy provides a useful foundation for approaching any type of challenge you may face as you guide your children. Although this book is intended for parents with young children, you will find that the techniques are ones that can be used throughout your child's growth and development..

Parenting can be a joyful occupation. We wish you and your family many years of happiness together as you grow and enjoy life together.

Susan Glaser, MA
Arthur Lavin, MD

W

Chapter One

KEY CONSIDERATIONS

*"There is always a moment in childhood
when the door opens and lets the future in."*
— Graham Green

A FUNDAMENTAL AMBIVALENCE

the moments after birth are precious. This is a time of extreme potential. Nearly anything is possible. The newborn can grow to be just about any kind of person. The parents start fresh, with any number of approaches to child raising available for their consideration. As parents, sometimes this time is experienced as one of tranquility—nothing has yet gone wrong. At other times it is informed by a certain anxiety—nothing has gone wrong, *yet*. Most of us have these and other powerful thoughts as we embark on the journey of parenting. Of course our feelings about parenting are also greatly influenced by the facts of the newborn's situation: healthy or ill, typical or unusual. But for any child, parents are forever balancing a sense of contentment with a sense of worry.

THE INEVITABILITY OF SEPARATION, THE DANCE OF CONNECTION

from the moment the cord is cut at birth, children and their parents become engaged in a struggle to balance the craving for closeness and the need for distance. Like partners in a dance, the parent/child unit must negotiate the various steps needed for this process to unfold successfully. As in a dance, the process does not proceed in a straight line but with many twists and turns and steps forward and backward. Separation does not just refer to being physically apart; separation also refers to the child's development of his own personality

> For any child, parents are forever balancing a sense of contentment with a sense of worry.

and needs, independent of his parents. A large part of parenting in the early years is encouraging the child's innate urge for independent behavior while still conserving the boundaries that will help the child feel secure as he strives to become his own person. The dance of connection and separation is lifelong, and one of a person's central experiences. As such, the balance between connection and separation is also one of a person's most complex experiences. If the balance is always dynamic, the experience will inevitably reflect the culture in which it takes place. That is, in every community and in every era, a particular style in managing this balance is common to most families. Expectations from parents as well as children are an important feature of each of the hundreds of varieties of human cultures, varying between broad ranges of particular ethnic communities and historic periods. In modern America there has been a very strong emphasis on the *culture of caring*. At the same time, modern American cultural history has lost much of its trust in a wide range of sources of authority. Our observation is that although much of the loss of trust in authority may appear to be primarily in the business and political realm, it has a strong impact on the experience of family life, as well. Currently, parents' lack of trust in the very nature of authority helps bolster the view that to create a loving, caring family the must avoid the imposition of what they consider *authoritarian* rules.

One aspect of parenting that seems to transcend any particulars of a community's style of managing separation and connection is that the process is always imperfect. Adults and children cannot avoid striking wrong notes, and frequently. Fortunately both parents and children have a powerful interest in the process ultimately succeeding with our children emerging as effective, loving and successful adults.

perhaps one of the most common areas in which parents in our time and place struggle is the inevitable conflict that occurs as their infant develops into an independent, mature individual. Their belief that avoiding conflict is in the child's best interest may rob their child of the necessary struggles that help him differentiate himself from his parents. The effects of the avoidance of conflict often confound parents, as it leads precisely to the type of behavior that they had hoped to circumvent.

THE FUNDAMENTAL NATURE OF CONFLICT

the development of the child's own perspective is one of the most inescapable tensions of parenting. As the newborn grows, he or she progressively asserts him/herself as a new person with new needs, interests, and demands. Some of these new needs will be congruent with the parents' needs, and some will not. When the child's desires are not congruent with the parents', a potential conflict is born. By conflict we mean simply a difference of purpose that is not *obviously* resolvable. However, conflict is not necessarily unpleasant, protracted, *un*resolvable, or traumatic.

Our goal is to emphasize the normal aspects of conflicts that arise between parent and child. Our aim is to help parents learn how to see conflict as an important and valuable opportunity for their child's growth by giving specific guidance on managing particular examples. In this way, parents and children can learn to resolve conflicts. Our method allows parents to respect and recognize their child's needs and wishes while still establishing boundaries and setting appropriate expectations.

Cultures vary quite widely about what sort of issues typically lead to parent-child conflict, and about how the conflict is managed, but the fact that conflict occurs appears to be universal to humanity.

> Our goal is to emphasize the normal aspects of conflict: to see conflict as an important and valuable opportunity, with specific guidance on managing particular examples, so that you can both respect and resolve conflict with your young children.

TRADITIONAL VERSUS MODERN FAMILIES

a major distinction in the style of various communities' cultural responses to child-parent conflicts exists between traditional and modern families. This distinction may help clarify the nature of our modern style of parenting. Traditional societies tend to have recurring patterns of response to expected patterns of human life. In traditional societies, the ambivalences of parenting are responded to, in part, by the traditional expectations of what the family should do with children's requests at various ages. Community traditions inform each parent when to pick up a crying child, how to toilet train, and the correct approaches to discipline. Certainly family dramas occur, but they do so in the context of expected responses to the typical ways in which children have challenged their parents for millennia.

In sharp contrast, the modern family looks to its own insights to solve its individual problems. The actions of previous generations become more suspect than sacrosanct.

A key feature of the modern perspective is the role of insight from scientific observation and experimentation. All families in every era want to hear what other families have tried. However, in traditional societies, what has been done is the main source of counsel and advice. In sharp contrast, our modern families may be more interested in what has been learned from the fields of psychology and pediatrics than in what our grandmother did with her children. The modern family wants to do their own research and to find their own solutions. Rather than the actions of previous generations being a guide, it is their own up-to-date knowledge that guides their decisions.

> The traditional era offered clear guidance on the application of parental authority. This book provides approaches specific to our modern, nurturing era on how to apply parental authority while maintaining a caring, sensitive stance to parenting.

The shift from a traditional to a modern approach releases families from the bonds of past practice, but also removes the comfort of having past practices readily at hand. Now each family must find its own solutions to the challenges of parenting. For modern American parents, one of the greatest challenges is parent-child conflict.

We do not propose to settle this challenge with an appeal to return to the days of tradition. No society has successfully solved its problems by fully re-creating a halcyon past. Resurrecting the way things used to be never seems to offer a lasting solution to problems faced today.

Nor do we propose to simply call for authority to overpower nurturance. The interest families have developed in being caring, loving, informed, and nurturing is a great step forward, and we would be very unhappy to see that interest blunted to any degree. Our purpose, then, is to discuss how best to manage the use of authority in a family committed to being nurturing.

THE MODERN FAMILY AND CONFLICT

the fact that conflict occurs at times between all children and parents is widely known, but bothers many. The modern American family takes pride in a certain level of educated nurturance. Many American parents come to parenthood hopeful that they can anticipate and provide for their child(ren)'s needs sufficiently well to avoid any significant disappointments or conflicts. The last century has seen an explosion of research and insight into the realms of child development and human psychology. Armed with this new knowledge, our generation proposes an unspoken pact with each of our children: if we offer a nurturant, understanding approach to responding to their needs, then they will not pursue needless conflict. Underlying this pact is an unspoken hope: if we apply the best of modern knowledge to our parenting, then we can raise children free of the difficult pains of childhood we experienced; we can raise children ready to enter adulthood free of a troubling past.

> The modern family is based on an unspoken pact: *if* the parents provide the most caring and insightful approaches to meeting their children's needs, *then* their children will be content and the family will be relieved from conflict.

Therefore, it is deeply disturbing to many parents to realize that conflict itself appears to be an important part of normal child development. Ironically, it appears that conflict with the most trusted people in the child's life is the most important and helpful. For most children, the most trusted people are their parents, and so it is with parents that the conflicts are most sought after. This explains the familiar phenomenon of children being their most provocative with their parents, and acting so nicely with teachers and playmates. From this perspective, it makes sense that children will test their parents more than anyone else. Who else can they trust to react with love to their deepest resistances? Who else can they trust will not harm them when they act their most provocatively? **But the main point is that *children need to resist, to provoke, to conflict.*** There appears to be no other way for young children to learn what their world really can tolerate and how they can effectively take their own place in that world.

> That conflict *itself* would be an important aspect of childhood development is deeply disturbing to today's nurturant parent.

another key feature of how testing and provocation are central aspects of childhood behavior is repetition.

Children (and adults) appear to need to actually experience the limit of the acceptable many times before really understanding and accepting what that limit is. For example, many adults need more than a posted speed limit to believe that is truly the acceptable limit to car travel. The same is true of the child who is told not to do a prohibited action. Parenting requires a staggering amount of repetition. Rules rarely take hold without repeating and enforcing them many times.

> Repetition is a core requirement of learning rules, limits, and expectations (at any age).

And yet, this essentially biologic imperative for children to test their parents violates the two unspoken premises of a nurturing parent:
1. To anticipate the child's need in an effort to avoid conflict;
2. To avoid conflict to eliminate the presence of any trauma to the child.

The nurturing parents' commitment to conflict avoidance and fear of trauma is unnecessary and paralyzing.

the nurturing parents' commitment to avoiding conflict and their fear of trauma is unnecessary and paralyzing. It is unnecessary because conflict is a healthy, normal, and necessary part of life, and it is paralyzing because it creates a tremendous burden of guilt on any parent who tries to establish even the most reasonable limits.

In fact, not only is conflict an unavoidable aspect of childhood, it serves highly valuable functions.

As discussed earlier, conflict is an essential part of a child developing his or her own sense of self, but it also helps define what the acceptable choices are when developing that sense of self. An argument can be made that what defines major aspects of a culture's style is defined by what truly upsets one's parents. In many ways, what

Conflict is an essential part of a child developing his or her own sense of self, but it also helps define what the acceptable choices are when developing that sense of self.

makes the style of southern French culture distinct from the style of East Kenyan culture is the set of what behaviors are desirable and what behaviors are discouraged. We learn the very basic and most strongly held preferences of our own cultures at a very early age, and primarily from our parents. We would propose that children pay far more attention to the strength of their parents' response to their testing behaviors than to the words used by parents. It's when our parents care most that we believe that rule is the most important to learn. From this perspective, children can only learn what their parents really care most deeply to teach them by observing what violations carry the most weight. Without violating the rules, the strength of the rules is never tested or learned. As adults we all know which rules are always enforced and most important to observe,

Therefore, it is unrealistic for parents to think they can anticipate their child's needs to the point of eliminating all conflict.

and which rules are technically in force, but widely ignored. Our children seek that same knowledge, but require some testing of our rules to really know what counts.

When parents simply recite a rule but avoid repeating or enforcing it, the child learns that rule is not important. And so, if children can only fully understand their culture by fully testing the limits of acceptable behavior, even the most patient and indulgent parents will experience conflict with their child, *because their child will seek that conflict as an essential tool to understanding his or her world.* Therefore, it is unrealistic for parents to think they can anticipate their child's needs to the point of eliminating all conflict.

DISAPPOINTMENT AND TRAUMA

if we as caring parents would like to avoid conflicts with our children, we also fear that conflicts might be damaging. This issue will be more fully discussed in our chapter on managing sleep in infancy. The distinction between disappointment and trauma, however, is important enough to consider now as well. A vast distinction lies between the upset of a child denied his wish and the agony of a lasting trauma. If the parent's stance is reasonable, and the child is simply upset at not having things his way, the cry is one of disappointment, not trauma. Traumas are generated by unreasonable, terrible events that leave the child not only disappointed, but damaged. Disappointments are transient, with no harm done. Traumas force children to fundamentally reconsider whether the world is a trusting place, often with long-term consequences.

Disappointments are caused by reasonable limit-setting; traumas are caused by unreasonable harm. Few experiences could be more different.

However, for any parents who believe their child's disappointments are fully preventable and/or traumatizing, any such disappointments are intolerable. This paralyzes the parent from setting a limit, for fear of provoking a disappointment that the parent, in turn, will experience as a trauma for the child.

The final irony is that not only is conflict actually a normal, productive part of child-parent life, but so is limit-setting. In fact, children will seek their limits, challenging parents until the limit is set. And so parents who avoid setting limits will often experience their children acting increasingly provocative, until the limits their children seek are finally set.

The thought that a simple disappointment could be actually a trauma is a key source of parental paralysis in our nurturing homes. Nurturing is essential, but paralysis is unnecessary and harmful. Our advice is designed to preserve nurturing and eliminate paralysis.

Disappointments are transient with no lasting harm, and are a constant and normal part of life. Traumas are damaging and, of course, need to be avoided.

MODERN AMERICAN PATTERNS OF CONFLICT

HARSHNESS AS A FAILED STRATEGY

when considering modern American patterns of conflict in families with young children, we intend to focus on the issues that children bring to their parents for help resolving. We have little or no interest in trends amongst adult Americans that foster an interest in being authoritarian. Many societies, including our own, frequently lapse into a perspective in which harshness toward children is a virtue. Variously described as "the school of hard knocks," or "the strict father approach," or "a firm tradition solves all," these perspectives ironically avoid conflict, too. Any approach based on the assumption that adults must impose their will on a child, with no thought for what the child's desires are and no thought toward how best to thoughtfully resolve the impasse, flees from managing the conflict as surely as the approach that would grant the child his or her every desire. Our proposition is that young children reliably challenge their parents with desires that run counter to both their parents' and their own interest, and that knowing the most common patterns of such challenge allows parents to effectively craft responses that allow them to remain nurturing, to be thoughtful, and to be effective parents. In the process, parents then are able to avoid either the pitfall of always following their child's lead, or the pitfall of settling disputes by simple force.

THE MOST COMMON POINTS OF CONFLICT WITH YOUNG CHILDREN

for young children, a number of issues seem to recur in modern American culture as points of conflict with their parents. The nature of the conflict ranges widely in each situation, and is determined strongly by both the child's personality and the parent's responses. Despite the wide range of intensity and resolution of these conflicts, a relatively simple number of conflicts tend to present at least some challenge to parents:

- Sleep
- Feeding
- Discipline
- Toilet training
- Sibling rivalry
- Child care and preschool separation issues

At the heart of each of these conflicts is a **negotiation**. The child wants this outcome, the parent wants that outcome, and both weigh in, hoping to prevail. **The side that cares the most at any point in time usually wins.** We would propose that it is essential to know what you are negotiating if you hope to resolve the negotiation in your favor.

So, let's take a look at the core negotiations that underlie each of these most common parent-child conflicts of early childhood:

SLEEP
The child's desire:
To not sleep alone.

At every age, nearly everyone dislikes sleeping alone. Infants and children are no exception. They love their parents more than anyone, and want to be with them, even while sleeping. At the very least, they would like to just see their parents if they wake up in the middle of the night.

The parent's desire:
To have an uninterrupted night of sleep.

To have some time and privacy away from their children.

Of course, some parents like having their children in their beds. For parents who enjoy the family bed, there is no conflict for both sides are seeking the same goal.

FEEDING
The child's desire:
To have fun winning a struggle.

If a parent cares what a child chooses from her plate, it is too easy an opportunity for a child to say no and win a fight. Winning is fun at any age, but for a young child, prevailing over a parent is exhilarating.

The parent's desire:
To get the child to eat what is perceived as a physically important nutrient.

This is an unnecessary conflict easily resolved.

DISCIPLINE
The child's desire:
To do things their way.
To control the outcome of daily situations
and to figure out how much the parents care
about the rules they wish to enforce.

The parent's desire:
To ensure their child's safety.
To teach him or her the most important rules
of the culture regarding social learning, with
the end result that the child will be a successful member of society.

*This conflict is essential, valuable, and un-
avoidable.*

TOILET TRAINING
The child's desire:
**To have someone else do the work of clean-
up and to retain a piece of their babyhood.**
Particularly after age two and a half, children
are aware that diapering is a good deal, someone else cleans up the mess, and many (not
all) resist using the toilet and assuming responsibility.

The parent's desire:
To have the child take care of his own mess;.
To no longer have to do the clean-up; to help
the child take the first giant step toward becoming more independent.

CHILD CARE DILEMMAS
The child's desire:
To stay with the parents and play.
To engage with them instead of their teachers; to express their feelings of loss when left by their parent.

The parent's desire:
To offer the child a new opportunity to establish friendships.
To learn within a structured setting; to have a break from 24/7 parenting; to be able to work knowing that their child is in a safe, loving environment.

Although all children have these feelings, this conflict is highly variable, and some children do not express it.

SIBLING RIVALRY
The child's desire:
To express their resentment about the usurper in the family who drains away parental attention.
To have some fun; to preserve their status in the family; to punish perceived hurts and to learn how to exert their will in the world.

The parent's desire:
To have peace in the home.
To establish life-long sibling friendship.

OUR PURPOSE

we present this book to help parents understand the context of their conflicts with their children, and to share approaches to these specific conflicts that will make their parenting experience more effective. Our goal is neither to eliminate conflicts between child and parent, nor to find ways to distract children away from their role in resolving these conflicts, nor to seek authority by force or imposition. Rather, we see the conflicts of sleep, feeding, discipline, toilet training, sibling rivalry, and formal programming as opportunities for children and their parents to learn how to manage differences of purpose.

Rather than challenge our generation's loving commitment to nurturing, we intend to inform that commitment with a more nuanced appreciation and specific details on how best to use authority.

We offer a perspective in which caring parents can still exert input. We support the goal of being nurturing. We see nothing contradictory about guiding and caring. Our purpose is not to challenge our generation's agenda away from a caring, nurturing style. Rather, we intend to inform that style with a more nuanced appreciation for the role of authority in a caring family. Caring and loving parents can still establish rules and set limits. Limits are a response to the child's pursuit of conflict, not of the parent's desire for conflict.

if we succeed, parents who read our book will have a better understanding of why their child tests their rules, and how to respond specifically to the challenges of sleep, feeding, toilet training, discipline, sibling rivalry, and formal programming.

Chapter Two

SLEEP

"…the innocent sleep,
Sleep that knits up the raveled sleeve of care,
The death of each day's life, sore labor's bath,
Balm of hurt minds, great nature's second course,
Chief nourisher in life's feast."
— Shakespeare, *Macbeth*

sleep remains a mystery. All people sleep, and all people feel the need to sleep every day, spending roughly a third of a lifetime asleep. And yet to what purpose? Is sleep simply a physiologic cycle that we cannot avoid, or a state of mind needed for completion of our daily thoughts and desires? Is sleep an intermission from the main action, or is sleep our natural state interrupted by the necessity of wakeful activity?

Whatever the nature or purpose of sleep, however, it is clear that nearly all parents experience their first sustained conflict with their child over the issue of sleep. Perhaps all parents have had nights of less sleep than they wanted. Certainly, there are a number of fortunate parents who never experience any conflict with their infants over the issue of sleep. Some infants glide into nights of uninterrupted sleep early in life with little or no interventions from their parents. For other families, parents feel no strain being awakened at night for extended periods of time. But for a large proportion of parents, they experience long periods during infancy and toddlerhood desperately sleep deprived, anxious for their child to "sleep through the night," aching for a time when the whole family can finally receive the rest they need. It is the tension between the parents' desire for adequate sleep and the child's desire to have her parents available at any time of the night that creates the conflict over sleep. For parents that experience that tension, we offer our thoughts in this chapter.

if parents feel an urge to have their infant sleep through the night, it is the tension between the parents' desire for adequate sleep and the child's desire to have his or her parents available at any time of the night that creates the conflict over sleep.

NORMAL SLEEP PHYSIOLOGY

to deal effectively with the struggle over sleep, it is best to understand the normal cycles of sleep. Despite the differences between adult and infant sleep patterns, there are some basic similarities. Perhaps most surprising is the fact that infants and adults come close to waking several times a night. Our sleep is actu-

Everyone at every age wakes or very nearly wakes several times a night

ally a recurring cycle of varying phases of sleep, with recurring moments of near waking every night. As we fall asleep we leave consciousness and enter into a period of light sleep. The initial phase of light sleep typically lasts half an hour to an hour, and proceeds to the initial phase of deep sleep. Deep sleep tends to last one and a half to two hours before a return to another round of light sleep, which in turn yields to a moment of near-waking. If one falls back to sleep, the cycle of light to deep to light sleep recurs. Overall this complete cycle lasts two to four hours and is completed two to four times per night.

It is at the point of near-waking that a *critical* moment occurs: will the near-waker easily return to light sleep, or become fully awake? Most of us have had experiences that prove this recurring moment of near-waking. We are normally so adept at returning to light sleep that we spend most nights unaware that we come close to waking two to four times a night. However, when we fall asleep under altered circumstances, we do not re-enter light sleep and awaken fully. This explains how we can fall asleep with a light on or the radio playing but at other times find the same stimulation wakes us from what we perceive as a deep sleep. What is really happening is that the radio or the light did not wake us; it kept us from entering our next sleep cycle.

DEVELOPMENTAL ISSUES IN SLEEP, OR WHY A NEWBORN DOES NOT SLEEP THROUGH THE NIGHT

at the start of life, infants are born unable to sleep all night without interruption. The main reasons for this physically challenging fact are related to nutrition and sleep development.

NUTRITION
a person grows faster at birth than any time after birth. The newborn, starting at less than two feet tall, grows at an annual rate of over one foot per year! Compare this to the growth spurt of the ad-

olescent, already four to five feet tall, growing at less than half a foot per year. The initial rate of weight gain is roughly one ounce a day, which translates to a rate of gaining roughly 24 pounds a year, with a starting point of five to nine pounds at birth! These rates of height and weight growth slow considerably as the first year progresses, but these are the rates in the first weeks of life. This staggering, explosive growth of the newborn requires an equally incredible amount of food. The bare minimum is 45 calories per pound the baby weighs, but the typical might be double that amount. If an adult ate as much as many newborns eat per pound of body weight, the adult would need to eat 7,000 to 15,000 calories per day. Few adults could possibly eat this much. The only way a newborn can eat this much is to eat very often. This is the first reason young infants wake up throughout the night: to eat. Parents of a newborn have no choice but to wake up to feed their baby who needs more food every few hours.

> The first reason babies wake up at night is that in early infancy they need to eat.

Therefore, to reach the point at which babies will sleep all night without waking their parents, the baby first needs to have grown to the point that frequent nighttime feedings are no longer necessary. They must be old enough to grow at a far slower rate than at birth.

The age at which babies will have enough extra reserves to slow their rate of growth, and no longer need to wake several times a night to eat varies widely. This leads to the familiar experience of one family sleeping well with a two-week-old newborn and another still up frequently with a nine-month-old infant. By four months of age, however, a very substantial majority of babies will be large enough and growing slowly enough to sleep through the night without requiring nighttime feedings.

THE DEVELOPMENT OF SLEEPING SKILLS

the second reason that infants wake up frequently at night is that nearly all people are born unable to re-enter the next sleep cycle without fully waking. That is, when young infants are placed in the crib, they require help calming to get to sleep or to return to sleep as they enter another cycle. If parents do not help their babies develop the skills necessary to calm themselves back to sleep, it is unreasonable to expect them to be able to sleep through the night without parental involvement. It also turns out that four months is the age at which a substantial majority of infants have developed the ability to soothe

> The second reason young infants wake at night is that they cannot get back to sleep on their own.

themselves to sleep. Very few infants are unable to get to sleep on their own after reaching the age of four months.

THE CROSSROADS OF DEVELOPMENT AND CHOICE

once a baby (or, it turns out, any person) develops the requisite skills for a new task, he reaches a decision point, a crossroads. Will they advance, performing the new skill, doing more work, taking on new responsibilities, and gaining new privileges? Or will they choose to hesitate, remain in their already known world, safe, with less work and more help, but less independent, less productive? The nature of human life is that these tendencies are typically in some balance. We adults do not always drop our old patterns and assume our new skills without ambivalence. On the other hand, some steps forward are effortless and occur rapidly, while others are protracted inner struggles. So it is with infants and sleep. **For infants, the crossroads they encounter when they learn to sleep all night is whether to have a quiet, restful night of sleep, or to have the loving company of parents in the middle of night.**

> Babies over four months old do not need to be fed at night and have the capacity to get back to sleep on their own; the only reason parents are up with children over four months old is by their own

What is this choice a baby, who does not require food, faces when he or she wakes up in the middle night? *The choice is determined by the expectation the baby has upon waking: does she expect the parents to appear or does she expect to go back to sleep on her own?* All babies have the right to expect their parents will appear in the middle of the night for at least a number of weeks after birth, but at the point when babies no longer *need* their parents to feed or help them get to sleep at night, they no longer *need* to expect their parents to wake up to care for them.

Parents, in turn, also need to know when it is *necessary* to respond to their baby's cry at night and when they do not have to respond. Responding to all nighttime calls for help, even after babies can help themselves, can lead to a dramatic prolongation of the time during which parents do not get a full night's sleep. For most parents this adds several months of needless sleep deprivation. For many, the issue is not resolved for years.

For some families, responding to their infant during the night or allowing their child to sleep in the same bed is a satisfying experience and, therefore, no conflict exists. The following specific guidance is designed solely for the parents who feel conflicted about responding to their older infant crying several times in the middle of the night and interrupting their sleep.

DISAPPOINTMENT VERSUS TRAUMA

perhaps the greatest barrier to effective parenting around this issue is the fear that the baby's cry is a sign of trauma. We would like to draw a sharp distinction between trauma and disappointment. As noted in Chapter One, trauma is psychological damage; disappointment is simply a mood. By definition, trauma has a lasting impact.

> Trauma and disappointment could not be more distinct, and yet most caring parents experience the universal, natural, and healthy disappointments of their children as traumatizing.

Disappointment is nearly always transient. Trauma negatively impacts healthy development and naturally should be avoided whenever possible. On the other hand, disappointment is a normal part of everyone's life: it is not right or wrong, but an unavoidable part of living. Trauma is a harm created and delivered by one person to another person or the result of an avoidable event (e.g., the death of a parent). Disappointment is most often created entirely within our own minds; the result of our healthy, human drive to seek satisfaction as we bump into the unavoidable limits the world presents. The primary examples of infant trauma are abandonment, neglect, and abuse. The paradigm of disappointment is based in the frustration we feel when we cannot get what we want, when we want it. In short, trauma and disappointment have nothing to do with each other; they could not be more unrelated. Indeed, they are radically different events with radically different causes.

> Freud raised a new awareness that what happens in childhood can define critical aspects of adulthood, but he never claimed that each action of a parent was a potential mine ready to explode into harm to the child. Common disappointments are not such a mine, but rather healthy parts of life.

However, it is common for parents to confuse these widely disparate conditions. Why? Two forces seem to be at work: the history of psychology and the nurturant stance. Freud's insight that events in infancy and childhood could have a profound impact on adulthood launched a revolution in our thinking about childhood. No longer could society blithely ignore childhood as an immature stage of life that bore no connection to the fully mature adult. The depth of that insight remains vital to any consideration of our stance toward childhood. Some who came after Freud, however, exaggerated the potential harm that adults could cause to their children. While none would dispute the long-term consequences of trauma, too many have claimed that even the minor disappointments of childhood can lead to the same level of harm in adulthood. Today, many parents are taught either explicitly or by implication that infancy and childhood are a minefield of potential traumas. Just about any parental action that upsets a child could lead to a psychological cascade forcing the child to have serious adult neuroses, or worse. Of course our lives as adults are suffused with our past, but this does not mean any disappointments in infancy must be deemed traumatic. The Freudian legacy should not be parental paralysis, but rather a healthy respect for the psyche of any person, at any age. Our point is not to dismiss concern for the care of a child's mind and mood, but to truly value both by developing a proper place it into perspective. Not all unpleasantness is equal. To equate them all is to trivialize the actually traumatic, and to exaggerate the transiently disappointing.

the second trend that leads to this confusion is the nurturing stance. As discussed above, the nurturing stance is a valuable attitude that, like all attitudes, requires balance. In its extreme form, the nurturing stance demands an emotional monotone of happiness and contentment with a sharp avoidance of any range of emotional experience. No disappointment can be tolerated. This places parents in an untenable position, forcing them to accede to every demand of their children, for fear that they might be disappointed. An unpleasant feeling in one's child forces parents into a profound state of doubt regarding their own level of caring for their child.

> The acceptance of a place for disappointment allows parents and children to share the ups and downs of life with more flexibility and humor.

This makes the parent prey to unnecessary feelings of inadequacy, since all children experience disappointment. An unbalanced and extreme nurturing stance makes experiencing failure inevitable for the parent. The goal is to be sure that as parents we remain caring and loving, but with an open eye toward the natural, inevitable, and healthy place of disappointment in life. The acceptance of a place for disappointment allows parents and children to share the ups and downs of life with more flexibility and humor. When disappointments are tolerated, they lose their power. When disappointments are tolerated, conflicts shrink into their proper perspective. Troubles diminish, and healthy dynamics between parents and children have a better chance of thriving. Accepting that disappointments are a healthy part of life allows parents to be more confidently nurturing.

NEGOTIATIONS AND SLEEP

negotiations involve two or more people each seeking a different outcome, but forced to come to some conclusion about to what degree any or all will achieve their desired outcome. Negotiations resolve with a range of possibilities: one party gets his or her way and the other does not, or each party gets a part of his or her desired outcome.

Most struggles around sleep issues are clearly negotiations: the child wants to wake the parents up and be with them; the parents want to sleep. Only a limited number of resolutions to this negotiation are possible:

- The child is regularly able to wake the parent(s) and have them respond to him or her in their bed or come into the nursery every night.
- The parents are not available at night, and when the child wakes, he or she goes back to sleep without waking the parents.
- The child is able to wake and be with the parents for select situations, such as during travel or illness.
- The child and parents sleep together, and when the child wakes, very minimal activity of the parents satisfies the child with out fully waking the parent(s).

We would suggest that any of these situations, if acceptable to both infant and parent, is a healthy and sustainable approach to managing your infant's sleep. There is no particular virtue to any one of these approaches over another.

However, if a family finds that any one of these situations is not working, then we have found the following approaches to be almost always helpful in moving toward a resolution of the family sleep issue. A key point is that as long as the parents approach the waking child as a negotiating partner and not a desperate child, then whatever decisions are made will be more likely to be tolerable. For any outcome that upsets the child, the upset can then be seen as what it is: simply disappointment and not trauma.

> The cry of an older infant waking in the middle of the night may sound like the cry of trauma, but is actually simply disappointment.

To emphasize this important point, the desperate crying heard (particularly in a waking older infant), represents the disappointment of a negotiating partner not getting his or her way, and not the trauma of a damaging loss or catastrophic abandonment.

Janice and Rick have a 9 month old son, Robert. Robert is a sweet-tempered child who wakes to nurse three times a night. Janice and Rick expected to be up at night when Robbie was first born, but are now feeling exhausted. Robbie goes down to bed just fine, but at midnight, 2 a.m., and 5 a.m., he wakes up and cries until Janice comes in to nurse him. Even if he cries for a long time before Mom appears, Robbie falls back to sleep within minutes of nursing. Janice and Rick feel as though they should attend to Robbie's needs, and feel as though his crying is a sign of pain and distress that cannot be ignored. His cry distresses them both for there is almost nothing is worse than hearing their son cry. But, at the same time, they are getting exhausted and finding it is more and more difficult to function during the day. They also are beginning to feel a little resentful that they attend to Robbie all day and get no time at night to rest and recuperate. They feel trapped.

In this vignette, the situation is not acceptable to all sides. Robbie is happy; his parents come when called. But Janice and Rick are physically exhausted and emotionally unhappy about it. In this commonly experienced scenario, the family is being forced to resolve a negotiation created by the conflict that their infant's demands have placed on them.

Now consider the negotiators' stances at the start of the sleep negotiation. The child has a tremendous advantage: total commitment with no ambivalence. The child's desire to have the parent get up and come in is a totally unconflicted desire. By totally we mean that the infant or child wants the parent to appear with every fiber of his being, and will do anything in his power to achieve that end, with no qualms or second thoughts. The main means children employ, especially in infancy, is the cry. Aside from crying or screaming, there are essentially no other approaches they can use to achieve their goals. Consider, by way of contrast, the older child who can get out of bed and wake up the parent, or sustain a good verbal argument about the virtues of seeing each other at night. In contrast, the infant's unrelenting and sorrowful cry is his only tool for waking up parents and getting them to appear.

The child throws everything they have to get the parent to appear. They child has no hesitation to do all they can to wake their parent.

Now consider the parents' negotiating stance: deep ambivalence. We are typically caught between the deeply felt desire to sleep and the equally felt desire to respond. Many parents of young infants truly suffer from this ambivalence, finding little satisfaction in either horn of the dilemma. Setting a firm limit can provoke feelings of guilt, but responding to the cries can lead to serious sleep deprivation.

> The parents are racked by ambivalence. They want to sleep, but feel just awful about not responding to their crying infant.

This difficulty in many ways is defined by the misunderstanding of just what is taking place, as discussed above. After all, if parents think that leaving their infant to find his own way to get back to sleep is traumatic, that his cry is the cry of a primal abandonment, then it would indeed be cruel and unreasonable to leave their baby to cry. Better to forego their own needs (to sleep) rather than harm their infant.

However, if the parents know that (a) their child is indeed fully able to get himself to sleep, that (b) the cry is one of desire and not need, and (c) that the cry is a negotiating tool, not a primal scream, then the parental ambivalence can be more easily resolved. Setting a limit the child can reasonably achieve allows the parent to work effectively toward everyone getting the sleep they need and desire.

PRACTICAL TIPS

determining when it is appropriate to set limits
The key is to watch for the baby's ability to put him or herself to sleep at bedtime. Nearly all infants will have this skill by the age of four months. Of course, prior to four months of age, the younger the infant, the less likely he will be able to get to sleep without your help. To find out when your baby has developed this skill, the test is what he can do when you put him to bed before he is fully asleep. It is reasonable to try this anytime you think he can, usually after two to three weeks of age. If hesitant, this step can be taken gradually, by placing the infant in bed when just shy of fully asleep for a few nights, then an additional five to 10 minutes before the previous nights' bedtime every two to three nights.

shifting caloric intake from night to daytime
The body tends to remember the timing of its eating, and appears to develop hunger at roughly the same time it has eaten the day before. Hence, some people have their evening meal at 5 p.m., others at 7 p.m. or 10 p.m. It is curious to note that people who regular-

ly have a meal at 10 p.m. do not get very hungry at 6 p.m., and vice versa. The same is true of your infant. If you feed him or her at 2 a.m. regularly, he or she will reliably be hungry at 2 a.m. the following day. Further, at any particular age most infants will take in a fairly constant number of calories per 24 hours.

Therefore, if you want have an uninterrupted night of sleep, your infant will need to eat his or her nighttime portions during the day. This is easy to achieve; the shift of eating from night to day is spread out over all the day feedings, allowing for a nearly imperceptible increase in each daytime feeding making up the difference.

If breast-feeding, you can try decreasing the number of night-time feedings one at a time by a number of techniques:

- Rubbing your baby's back or singing to her in an effort to comfort her back to sleep without feeding
- Having Dad or another adult comfort the baby to sleep to avoid the stimulation of your breast milk's aroma
- If you are comfortable using bottles, consider giving your baby your breast milk in a bottle, and slowly diluting it from night to night until it is basically water (see below)

If bottle-feeding, employ the dilution strategy:

- Choose the first night feeding you want to eliminate, and make the formula for that feeding either $^7/_8$ or $^3/_4$ strength
- If your baby takes it well and is satisfied, drop down by $^1/_8$ or $^1/_4$ strength steps until you reach water. At this point, your baby is no longer hungry when waking at this time.

setting the limit

Once you know your baby is able to get him or herself to sleep and you have reduced the number of nighttime feedings to the minimum that you could reach, then you know that the primary reason for waking is to see you. This is a powerful want, and a want your baby is used to seeing satisfied. As noted above, the only way your baby can achieve this desire is to cry loud and long enough for you to appear. To a large degree, it would be unreasonable to expect your infant not to call for you if you regularly appear when he does call. Unfortunately, there is only one way to change your infant's expectation, and that is not to appear when he calls. Only then will he

The last step in the change to your baby sleeping through the night can only be taken by your baby: when he or she no longer expects you to appear when he or she wakes up in the middle of the night.

not expect you to awaken and/or appear in response to his call.

The key to setting the limit is accepting that your child will be fine and that the only change taking place is in your infant's expectations.

A number of methods have been proposed to help your infant change his or her expectation.

Some involve simply waiting until she decides not to ask for you, on her own. These techniques work well when your infant spontaneously sleeps through the night, but they do not work so well if your infant continues to seek your company in the middle of the night.

Other approaches ask that you go into the infant's room after progressively longer intervals, gradually introducing the concept of you not being available at 3 in the morning. These techniques in some way prolong what is always the last step in such progressions, not going in for two nights as outlined below.

Over many years of observation, we have been impressed with the very high level of success with:

the two night technique:
- First be sure your infant is old enough to get to sleep on his or her own, and that no or very few nighttime feedings are still taking place.

- Once you are sure that these initial preparatory steps are in place, have the family (it is very important to let older siblings know what is happening) schedule two nights during which they will be prepared to listen to your infant cry. It is important to schedule these two nights: to prepare all family members and to be ready to hold your ground.

- Remember, the crying you will hear is the cry of disappointment, not trauma. For those two nights, your infant will be upset and even angry that his expectation is not being met. He will know that you are in the home, and the next morning will bear no ill feeling. But he will be mad at least for the first night. Again, he will be upset and disappointed, but not hurt.

- On the scheduled nights, place your baby down to sleep and do not come back in *at all* until wake up time. It is critical that you do not re-enter the bedroom at all during these two nights. If you peek in, your infant will be once again convinced that it is only a matter of crying long and hard enough to get you to appear. **If you want your baby to have a change of expectation, you must behave differently than your baby expects.**

- Since your infant is being disappointed, he or she may cry quite furiously, but this makes sense. After all, your infant expects you will show up, and on all previous nights you have appeared when she cried for you, so it only makes sense she will be disappointed when you do not. Therefore, you should not be surprised if she gets upset and tries everything in her power to have you re-appear. Remember, the crying during these two nights may go on for hours, but it is the voice of disappointment, not trauma.

- Nearly all infants, after two such nights, will sleep all night without interruption afterward. It is, once more, critical to know that they will sleep through the night *because they have changed their expectations.* They will continue to progress through two to four sleep cycles every night. They will continue to nearly or fully awaken two to four times each night. But because they expect you are not available when they wake up, they will now go back to sleep on their own.

once you have helped your baby sleep through the night, you may be surprised at how much better days and nights are. You will be rested and have more energy to offer your baby during the day. Your infant will also be better rested and often will be in better spirits. Further, you will have established a useful bit of authority in your loving relationship. Such a step is a powerful demonstration of how parents can set a limit that helps everyone, but it in no way reduces the parents' commitment to nurturing their child. This is a supportive and caring authority that helps lead your child toward choices most appropriate to meet both of your needs.

Janice and Rick decided they needed more sleep and tried this approach. It took them several weeks to agree to try it; Robbie's cries were too painful to bear. But eventually their exhaustion piqued their interest and increased their willingness to try. They formally scheduled two nights during which they would not go in to Robbie. For the 10 days before those nights, Rick was designated to go in to Robbie to calm him to sleep, so that he would wean off nighttime eating. Then they steeled themselves to wait out Robbie for two nights. By the second night,

*appearance. By the third night, he was sleeping through
the night. On none of the subsequent days did he appear
upset at either Mom or Dad; in fact, he seemed more
pleasant and better rested. Both Janice and Rick felt more
rested and pleased that their family was finally getting a
full night's sleep. They could enjoy Robbie even more
fully knowing that bedtime was no longer a battleground
of conflict and resentment.*

PREDICTABLE SETBACKS

many parents dislike going through this exercise, but nearly all are
very happy afterward, *for both the improved sleep and improved
parent-child dynamic.* Before embarking on this course, however,
be aware that you can expect certain setbacks. You should know what
these setbacks are so that you know how to respond, returning to
your hard-earned routine of good sleep for you and your infant.

The main predictable setbacks are:

travel
The stress of journey and, in particular, the changed proximity of
parents to the infant usually helps infants revert to earlier expectations of having parents available when they awake.

illness
It is always reasonable to comfort your infants and children when
they are in pain or suffering from an illness. The problem is after
recovery, when the child still wants you there at his or her waking
moments in the middle of the night.

ineffective limit setting
When parents cannot help but peek into the baby's room during the
two nights of limit setting, the infant usually does not drop the expectation that they will show up on subsequent evenings.

For each of these setbacks, the solution is to go through the initial steps of setting the sleep limit again. After two full nights of not
going into your infant's room, you will probably achieve a night of
sleep again.

THE FAMILY BED

as many people know, most infants in the world sleep with their parents, not in their own room. In the United States, the opposite is true; most babies sleep in a crib, in a room separate from their parents. In recent years, the family bed has gained popularity in our culture. Our goal is not to endorse either the crib or the family bed, but to note that in the family bed, the frequent nighttime wakings of infants can be little trouble for the parents, who simply roll over, feed, and everyone goes back to sleep. Although family bedding can make night feedings easier, a child in the bed can also be disruptive and parents are often confronted with the questions of when and how to move the child from their bed to his or her own.

Therefore, even in families where children start out in their parents' bed, the techniques in this chapter may become relevant to them at some time.

SUMMARY

newborns begin life with few routines that align with ours. They like to eat and sleep in short intervals. Within a few weeks to months, however, they develop the ability to sleep for eight to 12 hours without interruption. At the same time, they develop the regular sleep cycles of humanity, repeating this cycle two to four times per night, with each cycle including a near-waking experience. Most infants learn how to get their parents to wake up and come to them at their wake point in each sleep cycle. Many parents experience guilt and confuse their infant's *desire for company* with a *need for attachment*. Setting a fair limit on your availability will disappoint but never traumatize your infant. The disappointment may be loud but, if the infant is allowed to respond fully to changed circumstances, quite transient. Setting the limit almost never requires more than two full and consecutive nights of not going into your infant's bedroom, shifting his expectation so fully that he sleeps through the night without interrupting your sleep. This approach may need to be repeated after travel or illnesses. Families who sleep together with their infants may not be able to set the limit in the same manner, and may be able to

> successful resolution of a conflict with one's child requires understanding the specifics of the negotiation, and yields tremendous gains in well-being and confidence for both children and their parents. Sleep is but the first example of normal and healthy conflicts that can be resolved very successfully.

achieve a good night's sleep with very rapid calming of their infant during wake points in the sleep cycle.

Finally, the experience of successfully negotiating a conflict with a young infant illustrates how caring parents can guide their child by setting clear expectations, while remaining very nurturing. Parents routinely report that this balance yields improvements in home life, in the relationship with their children, and with their own enjoyment of family. These themes are realized in nearly every form of negotiation between child and parent. Once the point of the conflict is recognized, a successful resolution relieves parent and child, and allows both to feel a step forward has been made, enhancing everyone's sense of well-being and confidence.

Sleep often offers families the first opportunity to manage conflict and to set the stage for balanced nurturing. Sleep is the most common area of conflict in families during infancy. As the infant becomes a toddler, the area of conflict often shifts from struggles around sleep toward struggles involving toilet training, discipline, and feeding.

let us see how the same principles developed in our approach to managing conflicts in sleep can help families manage the conflicts raised in feeding, disciplining, and toilet training our toddlers.

W

Chapter Three
FEEDING

*"A man hath no better thing under the sun
than to eat, and to drink, and to be merry."*
— Ecclesiastes

the experience of feeding your toddler varies quite widely. As with sleep and toilet training, some children find their own way to manage feeding without any conflict whatsoever. Some children like to eat a wide variety of foods and eat sufficient quantities to allay any fears we might have as parents that they are not eating enough. Unfortunately, many families find themselves locked into ongoing conflicts at the table. Parents can easily become very worried that their toddler's approach to eating is either too narrow or is too little. Either the toddler is not eating enough nutritious varieties of food, or she is simply not eating enough volume of food.

As with sleep and toilet training, eating is a basic function that all infants and toddlers eventually master. However, it is also a basic function that can generate conflict that can persist for months, and in the case of food, even years.

The good news is that of all common parent-child conflicts, this is probably the simplest to resolve. For healthy toddlers, resolving fights around eating is simple because healthy toddlers cannot physically deny themselves the food they need. Once parents can be sure their toddler is healthy, the parents have an enormous advantage in this struggle, for the healthy toddler will always eat appropriately if no other option is available.

How then do families typically find themselves fighting with their toddler about eating? The typical way in which this problem presents to parents is that their toddler, who used to eat so well, is now fighting at every meal. Suddenly, the voracious infant seems to have gone on a hunger strike. Foods offered are routinely rejected, and frantic searches for something the child will be willing to eat often lead to a

> Of the most common parent-child conflicts, the conflicts over feeding are probably the easiest to resolve.

large jump in the frequency of serving "junk" foods. Even such desperate measures often fail, leading parents to go to bed feeling their child must be hungry, worried that his diet is loaded with unhealthy foods, and anxious that his growth will be stunted and his health impaired.

Let's take a brief look at the biology of eating, and then think about how to manage this conflict. This discussion will again be based on an overview of our general approach to thinking about behavioral conflicts with children: start with an understanding of what the child's actual needs are, think about what the child is actually trying to achieve, understand the specific conflict you may be immersed in, and only then establish an approach that respects the child's desire but achieves yours.

NUTRITION AND YOUR CHILD

nutrition is at once the most simple and the most complex task of parenting. Food must be provided for our children to be nourished properly. Every function of our body and our mind, including growth and development, requires the input of the right nutrients. No food, no growth, no functions.

There is no more compelling need our children confront us with. And could any need be more complex? Who of us is able to list each of the vital ingredients necessary for a healthy life, or in what proportion and amount they should be presented or eaten?

Not even the world's leading nutritional biologists could wake up every day and make a detailed list of the various proteins, fats, carbohydrates, vitamins, minerals, and other nutrients each of our children needs that day or week or month. And yet our children's health demands that they eat precisely what they need of each vital nutrient.

An important starting point is appreciating that the exact amount of food one needs on any day varies quite a bit, is a very complex calculation, and is reliably known by the body at any moment.

And so, even before any of our children protest, parents find themselves in a difficult position that seems to start from a position of profound uncertainty and risk.

Quite fortunately, the same biology that created a body dependent on food for sustenance also created approaches that allow the body to meet these complex needs as easily and with as little thought as we meet our needs for oxygen by breathing. The body constantly does its vital calculations and, unless disease intervenes, always finds the right answer. Thus, at any point in time, the body knows how much to breathe and how much to eat, and meets its most complex needs with little or no conscious calculation or even thought.

SPECIFIC PROPERTIES OF THE NUTRITIONAL NEEDS OF YOUR CHILD

let's think for a moment about what those needs are. Our children eat and breathe in order to provide their bodies with material that allows them to have sufficient:

- Energy (Calories)
- Material for brain, bone, muscle, and other tissues (protein, fat, minerals)
- Chemicals for vital metabolic processes (water, oxygen, vitamins, calcium and other minerals)

Each of these goals is so vital that, unless physical or economic disability intervene, every child's body is built to crave these materials until they are adequately ingested. **That is, every child's body forces him or her to eat until its needs are met.** In this sense, breathing and eating are quite the same activity: the body takes in material vital to its functioning, and is driven to do so, until that need is met.

> Every child's body forces him or her to eat until each need is fully met.

the second point to make is that for any particular child at any particular time, the precise amount of energy, material, and chemical matter needed is very hard to know, since it varies minute to minute, and day to day. That is, **just as we cannot know exactly how much oxygen our children need at any one time, we have very little idea of exactly how much food they need to eat at any specific meal or in a particular day.** And yet, despite the extremely vital need for breathing oxygen, we pay little attention to how much our children breathe in, and never battle them to breathe more. This is because we absolutely trust they will breathe what their body determines it needs.

and so the third basic point to be made is that just as we trust our children to breathe the right amount of oxygen, we should trust they will seek to eat the right amount of food. When offered food, children very rarely fail to take in the foods required to meet their energy, material, and chemical needs from food.

the last point of biology to make is that infants and toddlers have radically different needs for food based on the fact that they need radically different amounts. Newborns grow at an explosively rapid rate, but older toddlers barely grow from day to day. We grow faster when newborns than at any other time of life. As discussed in the previous chapter, shortly after birth, newborns can grow as rapidly as 24 inches a year. They will triple their body size in one year. Adolescents in their period of explosive growth only reach a growth rate of three to five inches a year.

Newborns triple the size of their body in one year; toddlers take many years to triple their body size. Newborns look visibly larger every day; toddlers look the same the next day. The different rates of growth are reflected in the growth curves at these ages. The newborn growth curve is steep; the toddler growth curve is nearly flat.

These differences are reflected in the difference in the intake of toddlers and infants. Newborns have to eat a tremendous amount of material to grow as rapidly as they do. If we ate as much as a newborn, an adult would need to eat roughly 7,000 to 15,000 calories every day! Toddlers are not growing that much on any given day, and so the extra amount they need to eat to apply to growth is a very tiny amount. As a result, toddlers need to eat just a bit more than we do, per pound of body weight. That is, the average 25 pound toddler needs to eat about one-third as much as a 100 pound adult. **And so, if we eat three meals a day, the 25 pound toddler only needs about one of our meals a day, of course distributed over the course of a day.** Children, like adults, vary in their food needs, and some toddlers may eat much more or even less than this amount.

The greatest nutritional threat to our children's health is excess, not shortage. Obesity is now rampant; malnutrition is quite rare without poverty.

finally, we should all realize that the number one nutritional hazard facing our children is not malnutrition, but obesity. Poverty is responsible for nearly all situations of restricted access to needed food, and neglect and abuse account for most of the remaining instances of malnutrition from lack of food. A vastly greater number of children, however, face nutritional hazards from excess eating, not from limited eating. **Most of our children are not at risk for missing food; they are far more at risk for drowning in food.**

MANAGING CONFLICT

many children eat quite well without any trouble, but many of our kids make mealtimes a time of intense conflict. The ways in which children can make meals difficult are relatively limited, but highly effective, and include:

- Refusing to eat what is offered
- Eating less than the parent wants them to
- Demanding a different meal or snack

William used to be a voracious infant, nursing for long times and with great frequency. Later in infancy he would eat seemingly unlimited amounts and varieties of baby foods, including all the vegetables. Soon after turning one, however, and despite great bursts of greater energy, William started refusing the great dishes his parents made for him. By the time he was 18 months old, he was refusing nearly every meal offered. Mealtimes became a frantic scene with Mom or Dad preparing dishes that were constantly rejected. Worried that William was no longer eating enough to meet his needs, an oppressive sense of impending doom drove William's parents to find something that he would agree to eat. In time, meals were reduced to a sequence of simple foods and sweets that William agreed to eat. Meals became either a monotonous provision of macaroni and cheese or a furious fight. William's parents began to worry that his growth or development might stall, stunt, or stop.

William's story is very common. And the approach to managing such a situation will once again illustrate key features of managing conflict, features that will be important in managing any conflict between what your child wants and proper guidance. Once again, we emphasize that conflict is a healthy part of life with your child. In the arena of feeding, the two strategies that essentially avoid dealing with conflict are giving in or being overly harsh. Giving in to food conflicts is easy— one just finds a goody to quiet the protest. The problem is that goodies are not a good basis for eating, and the child is left seeking some other approach to managing the conflict he ex-

These recommended approaches to feeding are designed to address the heart of the conflict — the fact that your child is seeking your help to resolve his inner struggle with himself and the outer struggle with you.

periences within. The other choice is to be overly harsh. Parents may yell at the table, punish, use coercion and force to avoid really managing the conflict the child wants so badly to engage in and resolve.

The following approaches are devised to address the very nature of the conflict. Your child is seeking your guidance and needs boundaries.

The crying and whining are merely the outward signs of this need. Even the most verbal toddler or preschooler is not articulate enough to tell a parent what he really needs.

FIRST STEP:
DEFINE WHAT IS NEEDED AND WHAT IS NOT

ONLY THE BODY KNOWS EXACTLY WHAT IT NEEDS
in this instance, what is needed is for William to have access to good food. What is not needed is for his parents to decide how much of that good food he should eat. Only William's body knows precisely what is needed for it to grow and function well each day. Remember from above that toddlers need far less food (per pound of body weight) than infants, despite their increased activity levels. We cannot know exactly how many calories, or grams of fat and protein, or milligrams of vitamins and minerals William will need on any given day. But William's body will know. Again, just as the body physically has no choice whatsoever in deciding whether to take in the necessary oxygen for a given day, so too is the body unable to deny itself the food it needs.

And so William's parents' job is to provide good meals to him, and then leave his body to decide how much of the food available really needs to be eaten. A good meal is a meal containing good grains, as well as good fruits and/or vegetables, and occasional meat and/or dairy. Over the course of a day, the total intake should include 500 mg of calcium, provided by any pair of the following: a cup of milk, a slice of cheese, or cup of yogurt; **or** 500 mg of supplement in the form of calcium chews (Tums, Vyactin, Flintstones).

SECOND STEP:
CONSIDER THE ESSENCE OF
THE CONFLICT WILLIAM HAS CREATED

WILLIAM WOULD LIKE HIS PARENTS TO DO HIS WORK
the heart of the problem in our scenario is that William shifted

responsibility for eating from his shoulders to his parents. William does not like his meal. And instead of William being the one to adjust, the parents are making the changes. Instead of William being upset, the parents are upset. Instead of William feeling the authority of his parents, the parents are responding to William's demands.

This causes two problems that can make meals miserable for parent and child:

- The child is sorely tempted to irritate his parents. Forcing others to change their plans or their mood, especially a powerful person, is too tempting to resist. In this case, power trumps hunger.
- The parent is caught trying to provide a solution that only the child can provide: making peace with what is served.

The point about power is critical to all our discussions about how to manage conflicts with your child. As noted above, children cannot resist the exhilaration, even though negative, of getting their parents to change their mood or actions. In this case it is greatly exhilarating to see a parent become very upset, cook a new meal, even yell.

Not only is the child's power expressed by his ability to impact on the parent, but also by the shift of responsibility from child to parent. In our scenario, a perfectly good meal is rejected by William. He has caused a problem. But instead of William being asked to find a solution to a problem of his making, the parents volunteer to take on the challenge. Our motives are admirable; we would like to help, but by assuming someone else's responsibility, we block them from solving what is, after all, their problem.

And so now we face the crux of the problem. We may think the key concern is nutrition, but often in these situations, the key concern is how can we remain caring, nurturing parents and still leave our children unhappy as they resolve their problems? The answer requires a balance of approaches: caring parents must remain very compassionate and loving and at the same time allow their child the space necessary to mull over, think about, weigh and consider her own challenges and problems. The proper balance should not be harsh; we are not advising parents to be unfeeling or to seek to impair their child's strength. Rather, we seek approaches that help parents lovingly provide their children the opportunity to find solutions to the problems they create. Our job as parents is not to hide the real

> The crux of the problem of food fights is not nutrition but power. The risk is not hunger for food but hunger for power.

conflicts our children seek to learn from, but to help our children learn from these problems in a caring and effective manner. Our recommendations help parents shift from struggling with food towards helping your child master their work.

Perhaps the best sign that a proper balance is struck is the element of humor. When we see William toss his food away, it is very appropriate for parents to take a step back and see what is really going on: a toddler has tossed his food. This is, in fact, sort of funny. The humor we are seeking is subtle. We are not laughing or mocking; instead our hearts are a bit warmed by the human condition. Like William, when we are caught by the need to figure something out, we may lash out. We love William, but will not solve his problems for him. We will warm to his efforts to do so, and smile a bit inside when he comes up with goofy solutions that do not work so well. We will be patient as he comes to realize this and seeks a better way.

We also know we are not responding well when humor flees in the face of dread or anger. In our scenario, the parents probably feel a tremendous amount of dread: will our child become malnourished, will growth slow or stop, will development be delayed? At the same time, as parents we might feel very angry: how dare he throw away the food I worked so hard to make? Why won't he just cooperate, at least just once?! Is he spoiled? Is he a brat?

THIRD STEP:
MANAGE THE CONFLICT

LET THE PARENTS DO THEIR JOB AND WILLIAM DO HIS
if the parents are assured that their toddler needs less food than imagined and that she or he *really* does want to eat what she or he needs and that she or he is not spoiled, then the parent is ready to think about how to manage the situation.

The Parents' Job
The parents' job in providing nutrition is very simple:

- Prepare good foods
- Present them in a way the child can eat them
- Nothing more

Each of these steps is worth considering.

in preparing good foods, we refer to the beginning of this chapter. Children should be fed mainly grains, fruits and/or vegetables with occasional meat or dairy items. Special attention to calcium intake is warranted as this is one of the few nutrients that children are frequently deficient in past infancy. Note that fruits and vegetables are equal nutritionally. There is no special virtue in eating vegetables rather than fruits.

in presenting foods, one should start with regular meal and snack times. These are times you can conveniently be available to prepare and serve the food. Setting these times limits your availability for such activity, a very wise step to take.

nothing more means just that. The parents are *not* responsible for making a child eat, or to eat a certain amount. Remember the oxygen analogy; parents are also not responsible for making a child breathe, or breathe a certain amount. So too with food. This step requires a critical **absence of action**: parents should not ever comment or push their child to eat a certain food or a certain amount.

The Child's Job
The child's job is also quite simple:

* To eat what he needs.

The Resolution
And so let's think about how to manage William's eating behaviors. In this scenario the parents will enjoy meal time much better if they:

* Prepare the meal
* Serve the meal
* At the first sign of refusal of the meal (**not** of a single food, or a bit of the whole meal) or of throwing the food, the meal is ended and cleared, and no further food is offered.

Again, this should be done with a smile, not with anger. This approach should be a matter of fact, not of feeling. When William gets angry or throws food, or shifts into total refusal, the parents can simply say, "Oh, are you done? OK, let's clean up then," with a lilt in their voice, and a smile on their face. The message is given, the place cleared, and the child allowed to leave the table. If William is unhappy about this turn of events, the parents should stay calm, not engage, let him know there will be food at the next snack or meal, and let William deal with his choices.

This simple solution has many varied and complex benefits. The first and foremost is that each member of the family now carries his or her appropriate responsibility: the parents prepare and present food, the child eats the food. Each member of the family no longer is responsible for roles he or she simply cannot fulfill; the parents are not deciding how much their child will eat, and the child is no longer deciding what food will be prepared and when it will be presented. And so, faced with being limited to deciding how much to eat, the child has no choice but to respond to a meal by doing just that. In nearly every instance, once the child's choices are limited to deciding what he has the most expertise to decide, he does an excellent job. The result is a calmer family table where everyone eats well, and where an important conflict has been resolved.

in managing the conflict of feeding thoughtfully and effectively, parents also achieve a number of other benefits:

- The end of an unending fight

- The reassurance that their child will be well nourished and that their child's nutritional safety is on firmer ground

- A step forward in their relationship with their child. Their child came to them with a problem, and the parent helped her solve it with great caring and much thought. The child learns that it is safe to bring real problems to her parent, and that her problems will be met with respect, caring, and real help.

- Trust is nourished. The child also learns that if he brings real problems to his parents loaded with strong and immature feelings, his parents are able to avoid answering with strong and immature feeling, and are able to maintain their stance as nurturing adults. The child learns essentially to trust his parents, just as the parents deepen their trust of their child.

SUMMARY

feeding our children is one of the most important functions of
parenting. The only other functions that compare in importance
are loving, teaching, supporting and protecting, and clothing our
children. For most of human history, feeding was a serious challenge,
food was often in short supply, and a major role of parenting was
preventing death from starvation. This appears to be an instinct that
has not faded as rapidly as the supply of food has eliminated the
threat of famine.

Despite the unprecedented abundance of food we now enjoy,
worries about adequate nutrition remain quite strong. However, the
greatest nutritional risk our children face today in
America is excess, not deficiency. With the exception
of calcium, nearly every other nutrient is typically in
excess in our children. Obesity threatens the lives of
over a third of our children, while malnutrition will
threaten the life of far fewer, mainly caused by the
scourges of poverty and neglect rather than adverse
choices by the child.

And so as parents it is important to approach the
task of feeding aware that when our children express
their preferences, assuming they are healthy and growing well, we do not have to worry about their refusals
of food.

Do not engage in struggles to make your child eat;
you can only lose. Our job as parents is to provide
food, and once served, our role has ended. If your child
does not want the food served, your role is very simple—clear the
plate and end the meal.

This simple approach offers the profound benefit of deepening trust
between child and parent by making clear each person's responsibility,
and allowing each to fulfill it in a caring and respectful manner.

This approach
offers the
profound benefit
of deepening
trust between
child and parent
by making clear
each person's
responsibility, and
allowing each to
fulfill it in a
caring and
respectful
manner.

our attention to the approach of engaging with your child with care
and respect in the effort to resolve conflicts will now turn toward
the issues and conflicts raised in the process of overall approaches
to discipline.

W

Chapter Four

DISCIPLINE:
THE GENERAL PRINCIPLES

"The art of teaching is the art of assisting discovery."
— Mark Van Doren

DISCIPLINE IS TEACHING NOT PUNISHING

to the nurturant parent, the very word *discipline* can cause anxiety and worry about what their actions can do to their children. Parents can experience many days and perhaps even *all* their parenting years at a heightened tension between the worry of being too lenient and the worry of being too harsh. Harshness conjures up images of being mean, causing harm, creating long-term traumatic damage. Being too lenient conjures up images of failing to teach the child the basic rules, fostering irresponsibility, encouraging further resistance, spoiling the child. Being too harsh is damaging and being too lenient is spoiling. With these choices surrounding parents, it is no wonder that approaching discipline often makes us feel that the stakes are large and we will more often than not miss the mark.

> Many parents experience discipline as a dilemma: they are forced to choose between being too harsh or being too lenient.

The dilemma perceived in having to choose between being too harsh or too lenient is complicated by another challenge: the illusion that love and caring will solve all conflicts around discipline. If parents accept the premise that conflict can be avoided if they just provide adequate nurturing and understanding, they may even blame themselves if their child "acts out" or does not comply with parental demands. Parents, paralyzed by the fear of doing the wrong thing, or feeling guilty that their child is upset, can end up acquiescing to the unreasonable demands of the young child. This, in turn, can lead to an abdication of parental rights and responsibilities.

> A common hope is that simply by being caring and loving one can avoid the perceived dilemma of discipline.

Perhaps the most powerful way to avoid feeling caught in a dilemma or in the grip of guilt is to once again consider that conflict is an inevitable and, indeed, healthy part of the developmental process. As we saw in the discussion of how to help your infant sleep and eat, conflicts are healthy and universal; it is a basic property of how we learn to master complex tasks as we grow and develop. And so it is with discipline.

At the heart of discipline are the rules we want our children to follow. Every culture asks its children to learn its rules. One could argue that cultures are distinguished from each other largely by the type of rules that they emphasize and most rigorously enforce. In fact, the more critical the cultural rule or norm, the sooner the culture wants its children to learn it. Some rules are learned without struggle or conflict, but nearly all children find at least one rule that they find objectionable and that they will resist following.

The heart of discipline is teaching our children important rules.

Sometimes the rule is resisted out of a simple preference; your child simply does not like what is requested of him or her. Sometimes the rule is resisted simply to resist. In the development of self, it is actually important for the child to try out resisting. The act of resistance helps children clearly define their own ideas and opinions and then (with parental help) learn how to manage their words and their actions.

The occasional distaste for a rule plus the need to resist as part of developing the critical sense of self, essentially guarantees that all parents will experience vital and healthy conflicts frequently during their child's lifetime.

THE CHILD'S INTEREST IN THOUGHTFUL, EFFECTIVE DISCIPLINE

although it may seem counterintuitive, even as children are actively resisting rules, they are also simultaneously looking to their parent for real guidance. The child who resists the imposition of a rule is a familiar sight, but what is not so obvious and just as universal is the hunger children have for guidance. The desire for conflict and the desire for guidance are intimately connected at several levels.

How can we know that children are looking for parental rules and boundaries when their behavior seems to indicate the opposite? At the most basic level, if the child had no interest in learning the rules, a very different sort of conflict about rules would be experienced. The child would simply ignore her parents' guidance, and the conflict would be rather one-sided with the parent searching for ways to engage their child. However, we all know that children's conflicts about learning rules are quite engaged, if not enraged. The child typically is quite aware the rule is important, and his negative reaction and/or resistance almost always reflect an intense struggle over how that rule will go. Children care as deeply as adults about the rules and conflict will naturally erupt when a difference of opinion about the rule arises, rather than simply because the child has no interest in the arena.

At another level, the act of resistance helps the child define how strong the rule is. Rules we care little about are enforced infrequently and with little feeling. Rules that we care deeply about — in particular, rules that protect our children's health and safety — are enforced at every turn and their violation causes immediate, intense, and deep feelings in the responsible parent. If we would rather someone put their shirt on before their socks, we are unlikely to enforce that preference with any sincerity. But if our child runs into the middle of the street, or tries to touch the hot grill, our response is dramatic and nearly instant and generates a profound feeling. Children are built to read how much their parents care about any particular rule, and are always keenly aware when a rule is deeply held by their parent. You might liken a child's resistance to being taught a rule to a carpenter tapping the wall to find the studs. The carpenter is tapping all along the wall to find the spots that have the hard wood support behind them. The child is jumping on all the rules to see which ones have the firmest support behind them. In this way, too, the child's eagerness to resist and to learn the rules are very tightly interwoven. Ironically, the same child who is such a discipline problem is also eagerly seeking answers about which rules really count, how to learn to live in his or her parents' culture, and ultimately how to live in his or her world.

> Children have a very deep and profoundly interwoven interest in both learning the rules and resisting accepting them.

AVOIDING THE ILLUSION THAT "ALL IT TAKES IS LOVE"

now we return to the key illusion that all parents experience in teaching their child(ren) the rules: the illusion that love and caring will solve all conflicts around discipline.

Love and nurturing are primal and universal needs for all children, but they do not take the place of active discipline and guidance. Many children who struggle with their behavior are loved unconditionally. These children have one important need met but lack another one: the need for parental guidance, boundary setting,

A key illusion: That love and caring are all that is needed to solve all conflicts around discipline. Love and caring remain central to parenting, but guidance (not harshness) is needed, too.

and discipline. At times parents can become so worried that their child will be unhappy if denied or if thwarted in her actions that they do not help her "learn the rules." Parents may temporarily avoid a conflict but they will not be conflict-free as their children will continue to push the envelope until they get some reaction. In fact, these children are often the most unhappy children professionals see. They are longing for their parents to take back control and their inappropriate behavior is the way they are letting Mom and Dad know that something is missing.

Being nurtured is a need that precedes all others, but once met, has little impact on learning rules. Learning the rules requires guidance and so the child who is only nurtured and not guided will have a great need unmet.

if we appreciate how deeply children seek guidance, and how closely this need is linked to the need to resist, then we can start thinking more clearly about the central challenges inherent in teaching our children the rules we consider most important. In this situation there are parents who want to teach the rules and a child who wants to know the rules but whose learning often must include testing and resistance. If this situation is understood, then conflict characterized by resistance and testing is to be expected and anticipated, but can also be managed by informed parents. The discomfort of feeling that choices are limited to being too harsh or too lenient is transformed into awareness that conflict is something the child brings to the interaction for good reasons. Further, these conflicts that the child needs to experience are a natural consequence, not created by the parents, and therefore, do not need to be resolved by them.

If a parent equates discipline with punishment, meted out as an unpleasant consequence for a behavior that violates the rules, then the parent will remain caught between a rock and a hard place. If the parents punish, they feel that they are being too harsh; if they don't punish, they feel they are being too lenient. It is important for parents to remember that discipline is not primarily about punishment.

Discipline is the art of teaching your child rules, and applying them in the face of his or her deep need to learn and equally deep need to resist. Discipline is indeed teaching, not punishing. Of course, sometimes teaching and applying a rule will include consequences, but in this perspective, the consequences are a tool to teach your child a skill that he can employ in the future, when faced with a similar situation. Parents often feel that if a punishment is not given, their child will not learn. However, many parents discover that punishment (or threat of punishment) may work to stop a specific behavior at one moment, but does not seem to prevent their child from repeating the undesired behavior in the future.

The techniques we propose will stop the behavior in the moment but, more importantly, also give the child tools to manage more appropriately in the future.

> Discipline is the art of teaching your child rules, and applying them in the face of his or her deep need to learn and deep need to resist.

EFFECTIVE LANGUAGE TECHNIQUES ARE KEY

parents will sometimes not act because they are uncertain how to verbally respond to their child. They know that they aren't going to yell or spank, but then what? There are specific language techniques that parents can use that will set clear limits but also take into account the child's feelings and inner conflicts.

Some examples of typical situations may help to clarify:

screaming at the grocery store

Lucy is at the grocery store with three and a half-year-old Randi who spies some candy she wants. Randi immediately asks for it and Mom says "No." Randi is thrown into an immediate conflict with her mother. Randi wants the candy and her mother does not want her to have it. Randi makes an inappropriate choice. She pulls on her mother's hand and starts to yell in a loud voice. Children quickly learn that tantrums in public places often gain them their prize. Mom has some choices. She can give in and quiet the crying. She can equal her child's anger and yell back, refusing the candy, which prolongs the tantrum and leaves everyone feeling unsettled. Often a parent will engage in negotiation or arbitration: "I'll buy you the candy but you can't eat it until dinner is over" or "If you can stop crying and be good for the rest of the shopping trip I'll get it for you then." Here children learn that a tantrum ultimately gets them what they want. Both of these choices leave the parent uneasy as she considers the dilemma between harshness and leniency.

> The solution is to teach, rather than threaten or negotiate, and to help the child resolve the conflict she created.

The solution is to teach, rather than threaten or negotiate, and to help the child resolve the conflict she created. A more effective alternative is to reflect back the wishes of the child while not giving into the demands. Lucy might say to Randi,

"I see that you really want that candy now and it's hard for you to understand why you can't have it. You are pretty mad that I said no, but it is not time for candy."

Sometimes just putting the child's wishes into words helps her calm down, but if Randi still insists, Mom can say,

"You are so mad at me for not giving you the candy that you are yelling. You know that a girl who is three has big girl words. I will listen to your words but not to your yelling."

At home, Mom could just walk away. In a store she will only be able to turn her back slightly and wait for the high emotions to wane. This alternative clearly takes the longest, but in the end Randi learned about a limit while still having her feelings accepted and validated. This example illustrates how creating a plan, having confidence in your position and stating it clearly allows you to teach and apply a rule without being either harsh or lenient.

Using this type of language takes some practice and requires keeping a cool head when your child has just pushed all your buttons. For most of us, it is like learning a foreign language. You may even feel self-conscious at first, but soon it will become part of your daily lexicon.

STEPS TO EFFECTIVE DISCIPLINE:
THE SPECTRUM OF DISCIPLINARY ACTIONS

although each child is unique in his or her own right, there are certain techniques that can be useful in many situations. It may be helpful for parents if they think of their responses as falling on a continuum; some children will positively respond after one or two steps; others will need more active intervention to bring the conflict to a resolution. At the beginning many parents will have to use all the steps because their child has to unlearn that crying, physical violence, and tantrums no longer work.

STEP ONE
Stop any inappropriate physical activity.

Get down to your child's level and make a gentle physical contact before speaking. This avoids the yelling-across-the-room syndrome, which many children learn to tune out.

Let us take the situation where a child grabs a toy from his friend on a play date. The first step is to quickly and calmly stop the action. Stoop down to your child's level, hold him firmly by the shoulders, make eye contact and tell him in a no-nonsense voice that grabbing the toy is against the rules. At this point you may have to put your hand on the toy to keep it from being used as a weapon and to keep both children engaged.

STEP TWO
Describe the behaviors you are observing.

This is one of the most difficult things for parents to do. Parents, often out of embarrassment or uncertainty, yell at a child or use threats when trying to discipline. On the other hand, some parents, worried about what effect their harsh words will have, say nothing. Remember this is the dilemma we often place ourselves in when thinking about discipline: too harsh or too lenient. To shift the focus from this dilemma, the key is to focus on teaching the rule you want your child to learn. Learning the language that describes a child's *mistaken behavior* takes time and may, at first, even feel awkward to you. In the above situation you might say:

- *"I see that you wanted the truck Mark had and you grabbed it. Look at Mark's face — he is sad and crying. I think you know what you need to do to make him feel better."* At this point, it is likely that you will have to make some suggestions, but amazingly even three-year-olds will soon be able to figure out ways to help their victim and, more importantly, begin to substitute more appropriate behavior in the future.

- Many parents force a child into saying "I'm sorry" or take the toy forcibly and give it back to the victim. This response helps neither the victim nor the perpetrator. A forced "I'm sorry" is hardly sincere and does not demand enough responsibility for an inappropriate action. A child who is helped to understand that his actions had negative consequences for another and now must make amends is learning an important lesson *that will transfer to other situations.* The child who is given the toy back by the parent has not learned how to get what he wants, but rather has learned how to be a better victim. A child who has been hit or had a toy grabbed away will be better served by learning how to express his needs and generate a solution. This means that the adult must model the type of behavior that will achieve the desired results.

- The adult will have to guide the children through this problem solving process in the beginning. An adult can empower the children by asking questions like, *"Can you think of way for both of you to have a turn? There is just one truck and two boys who both want it."* Children over three may surprise you. The child who grabbed may be so surprised that the adult understands his needs and has articulated them for him that he may simply hand the toy over. Other children are so invested in the conflict that the adult will have to *move down the continuum* and increase her intervention.

- A parent could give suggestions such as helping the children take turns or finding another truck. The younger the child, the more likely it is that the parent will have to help model the new skill. Obviously, there would be many alternatives and parents would size up the situation before making suggestions. For three, four, and five year olds, the parent can ask for suggestions from the children and then *wait* and see if they can work it out. This is different from a parent not responding at all and just watching from afar to see if the children can work it out themselves. By intervening with this technique, you have set the stage for these children and given them a job — to figure out how two children can use the same toy.

Not only do these approaches work, but they empower children and develops positive self-esteem by allowing them to be the problem solvers.

STEP 3
Help your child label the feelings
Sometimes it is obvious why a child is upset. Someone grabbed a toy, a request was denied, a knee got scraped. Parents can easily give words

to these apparent feelings. *"You got so mad when your brother took your doll. You are angry that you can't have candy right now."* By labeling these feelings, you are validating the child's reactions and helping him understand that big feelings can be described with words.

Let us say that Johnny does not want to leave the playground, even after several reminders and a two-minute warning. He becomes upset, cries, and attempts to hit his mother. At this point parents have several choices. They can give in to the demand and stay a bit longer. They can pretend to walk away, leaving their child behind. They can yell at their child and/or spank him. Or, they can respond to the feelings that are causing the behavior. Let's explore some of the ramifications of each of these choices.

- You allow your child some extra time. This may, in fact, be a viable alternative if you have the time, but if you consistently allow your child to dictate your schedule, the lesson learned is that tantruming gets the desired results

- Many parents find that simply walking away and saying, *"OK, you can stay but I am going"* usually gets their child running to their side. Although it works, there are problems with using this technique, as it strikes at the heart of one of your child's most central fears: being abandoned. Although the parent has no intention of leaving her child alone on the playground, the youngster does not realize this. The very *thought* that his parent would consider leaving him is damaging, as it erodes trust and it is based on an untruth between parent and child.

- Yelling or striking the child makes all parties feel out of control, and although the child may comply (with tears and indignation), no one really wins in this scenario. Using words to help the child identify his feelings and giving him an opportunity to problem solve may be more time consuming, but is very effective. In this case, the parent may say, *"Johnny, I can see you are having a hard time leaving the playground. You are having such a good time you are mad about having to leave. It's OK to be mad, but we need to leave now."* At this juncture, many children, so relieved to have their feelings understood, simply leave with the parent. If your child cannot do this, you will have to move down the continuum and actively intervene. You may give Johnny the choice of walking out on his own or being carried out. Many children will sit down or run away — the non-choice. The parent can then say, *"I see you made your choice — I am going to have to carry you out."* Some parents think this is a victory for the child, but if the parent remains calm and can tell him, *"I see today you could not leave on your own, but I think that the next time we come you will be able to walk out all by yourself."* The parent's words are powerful: if you are angry and engage in a tug of war, the child has learned that his actions really had an impact on you. If your words are chosen so that the child feels that his choice made *him* feel disappointed and that walking out would have made him feel more grown-up and more in control, then a valuable lesson has been taught.

STEP 4
Set your child up for success, not failure.
In this case, Mother warns Dolly, age four, not to throw the ball in the living room. She tells her that in a few minutes she will take her outside where she can play. A few minutes later, Mother hears a crash. She comes into the living room and sees a small, china bowl lying broken on the floor. It is not exactly a Ming vase, but Mother is understandably upset.

Many parents, so upset with this obvious violation of the rules, engage in an interaction that will inevitably lead to failure:

mother: *Did you break this bowl, Dolly?*

dolly: *No, I didn't!!*

mother: *I can see that you did! Why are you lying?*

dolly: *I'm not lying! It just fell off the table!*

mother: *Don't tell me that! I told you a hundred times not to throw the ball in the house because you can break something and that's what happened.*

dolly (crying now): *I didn't, I didn't.*

mother (yelling now): *Stop crying and help me clean up this mess! Then go to your room! You can't go outside and you can't watch television for the rest of the day!*

In this scenario, no one feels good about the outcome. Dolly has been backed into a lie, Mother is yelling, and the bowl is still broken. In a situation like this, parents need to decide what their ultimate goals are. A parent may say, *"I want my child to understand that there is a reason for rules, such as not throwing in the house, and I want her to feel some consequence for her actions."*

The parent above is using revenge and punishment to teach her child about listening and following the house rules. Again: **discipline is not punishment, it is teaching.** Is a yelling mother and a crying child the only way such events can unfold?

Consider the way the exchange might have developed:

mother: *(rushing into the living room upon hearing the crash):* *I see that bowl is broken, Dolly. I think you know that when balls get thrown in the house, things can get broken. I see that is just what happened.*

dolly: *I didn't mean to.*

mother: *I know you didn't, but the bowl is broken. You know what you need to do now.*

dolly: *Clean it up?*

mother: *That's a good start. But that was a bowl that Grandma gave me. How do you think she would feel about it being broken?*

dolly: *I could call her up and say I'm sorry. I could buy you a new one!*
(Most four-year-olds have the general concept of buying things, but little concept of how much things cost; remember it is the principle of the thing.)

mother: *Buying me a new bowl is one idea. It costs money to buy something new. Can you think of ways to earn some money to buy a new bowl?*

At this point parent and child could negotiate some chores around the house that would help to make up for the broken bowl. The main point of the interaction has shifted from punishment to teaching the rule. A punishment is present in both approaches, but in the screaming match in the first example, the punishment is essentially all that is offered. In fact, in the first scenario, the child is essentially dictating how the process will unfold. It is the error of the child that seems to force the parent into a highly charged response.

> The main point of the interaction has shifted from punishment to teaching the rule.

In the second example, the parent takes control of the situation. Now it is teaching a rule that defines what will happen. Follow-through by the parent is essential here, as well, as a firm voice and a neutral bearing. Even a four-year-old can do a simple chore around the house for a number of days to help her feel like she is making some sort of reparation. Dolly is not backed into a lie. She realizes that she must make amends and has to take responsibility for her actions. The parent can feel like she has helped her child take a giant step down the road of accepting her obligations.

It is likely that many parents will say that the last scene sounds great on paper, but will never work in real life. Without a doubt, learning effective language techniques takes time, patience, forethought, and some personal introspection. At first, using therapeutic language can even feel awkward for parents, but if used consistently, it becomes a natural extension of your daily interactions. Parents who have begun to use this technique report that they feel in better control because they have a plan of action. Their calmness translates to their children and results in more effective disciplining. Children respond more positively to a parent who is in control and who allows for the expression of strong feelings, even while forbidding the action.

> Effective language techniques are neither harsh nor lenient. Rather, they are effective because they allow parents to make teaching rules the centerpiece of their discipline.

Most importantly, effective language techniques are a key technique that will allow parents to make the job of discipline an effective form of teaching, again releasing us from the trap of feeling forced to choose between being too harsh and too lenient. Effective language techniques are neither harsh nor lenient; they are simply effective.

APPROACHES FOR WHEN YOUR CHILD
IS NOT RESPONSIVE TO THOUGHTFUL GUIDANCE

A thoughtful, well-expressed approach to teaching our children the rules can eliminate much of the frustration experienced when trying to discipline. However, most children need to actually push the limits hard enough that nearly all parents will find times when they simply want to break the rules no matter how clearly and calmly they are presented. So what to do when your child is not responsive to thoughtful guidance?

CHARLIE LOVES TO RESIST

lately it seems that charlie just loves to pick a fight. Every time his parents, Steve and Megan, ask him to do something, he digs in his heels and refuses. Sometimes four-year-old Charlie won't come to the dinner table, or refuses to get dressed, or won't stop trying to pick on his little brother, or sneaks into the pantry and leaves a mess. Steve and Megan are at their wits end and feel as though they spend all day yelling at Charlie or trying to ignore something that they find deeply objectionable. Charlie is a loving son, too. He loves to get bedtime stories, and loves to cuddle and sleep with Mom or Dad. He beams with pride when his parents are pleased with him, but often ends up crying after breaking some rules and getting yelled at. Steve and Megan have talked to their families, pediatrician, and nursery school teachers about Charlie and they get loads of advice, but none of it has worked so far. Some family members say that they should simply ignore him; others say he should be severely punished, including spanking. These suggestions leave the parents torn between feeling guilty for being too mean and then guilty for being too easy. The pediatrician has recommended using time outs, and the preschool teacher has discussed how to speak to him before the situation deteriorates. The advice seems to make sense but they are having trouble implementing it.

STEPS TO EFFECTIVE DISCIPLINE: BEING EFFECTIVE
IN THE FACE OF CONFLICT AND RESISTANCE

STEP ONE

Try to give your child opportunities to stop resisting.
Once your child has decided he would like to resist the rule being applied, there is an important issue of face-saving that would be wise to appreciate and, if possible, circumvent. Charlie might decide to

refuse to dress whenever he is asked to, so one might consider using techniques that will prevent him from feeling humiliated if he is forced to give in. These include **humor** and **distraction.** As the tension builds and both parent and child become aware that the rule is about to be tested, a moment might present itself where a bit of humor or a distraction gives everyone permission to go along with the rule without feeling any loss of power. A silly joke or a story told just as the time to dress approaches, a review of the exciting events of the day coming up, even just changing the subject, can give a child an excuse not to engage in battle with you on that day on that rule. Battles over daily rituals can become so expected that a distraction or different approach presented by the parent can help break the cycle.

STEP TWO
Make a list of rules that both parents feel reflect their priorities.
It may sound obvious, but one of the basics most frequently ignored is that the parents must have a consensus and an explicit listing of the rules that are most important to them. To make that list, both parents should sit down and agree on their top priorities in terms of rules of behavior they want their children to learn and follow. Some rules will be more important to Dad, some to Mom, but both must settle on a list they both agree reflects their priorities.

STEP THREE
Connect a consequence to each rule,
and the threshold for its application.
Once the rules are agreed upon, consider what sort of consequence is appropriate and at what point the consequence occurs. Consequences should be just that — events that occur when a certain threshold of violation is reached, not expressions of anger or punishing events. The goal is to teach the rule, not break someone's will or cause shame. (See the discussion of consequences that follows this section.)

STEP FOUR
Make the rules explicit.
Once the rules are defined, let the child know what the expectations are and exactly what the consequence will be if expectations are not met. For older children, you may even want to write them down for presentation. It can be a poster, or a book, or a computer screen, but it must be explicit, easily presented, and easily referred to. *When a rule is broken, refer to the list.* The reason for this is that it removes the parent directly from the conflict and minimizes the chances for a power struggle. If you have done the above steps, now you

gain the benefit of your hard work. **If distraction, humor, or other steps to avoid rule breaking fail, and the child insists on breaking the rules,** *let the rules indicate the response.* This allows you to teach and not scream. In the event of a rule being broken, the child is simply told to refer to the agreed list and read the rule. The consequence, if activated, is applied. This way the child has his resistance pointed more toward the rulebook and away from the parent.

THE GOAL OF USING THESE TECHNIQUES IS TO MINIMIZE ANGER AND SHAME AND MAXIMIZE LEARNING

remember that the point of discipline is teaching and that the child wants to both learn and resist. Consequences are designed to aid in teaching, and to avoid needless emotional confrontation, pain, and suffering. Too often when children break the rules, we feel a need to make them remorseful, to make them feel so badly they will never break that rule again. When safety is severely compromised, such as running into a busy street, then it is nearly impossible to avoid getting angry, and in those settings anger is an honest and productive response — to not be angry would be dishonest and would minimize the nature of the danger.

However, if someone like Charlie resists getting dressed or makes a mess in the kitchen, with some regularity, then the question is not one of sudden, unexpected danger. The question is how best to structure your daily routine in a way that allows your child to learn the rules without you becoming routinely angry and always trying to break your child's will.

Ironically, a steady, explicit use of consequences is the best approach to getting yourself out of the dynamic of angry punishment. With good application of consequence, it is the rule that is being applied to the child, not your anger. It is the consequence the child is struggling with, not you. It is the question of the rule the child is left to ponder, not his hurt feelings or sense of shame.

Consequences should be given soon after the rule violation and as much as possible should be a logical or natural consequence of the rule. Punishments that are applied too far in the future will have a diminished impact on the child's behavior.

LOGICAL OR NATURAL CONSEQUENCES OF RULE VIOLATIONS

most parents understand the logic of having a consequence that is tied to the rule, but find it difficult to apply these consequences. One of the reasons for this may be that the parent feels the need to take away something of value from the child. It is hard to break away from the notion that a child can only learn the rules if he is made to feel shame, sorrow, or pain. But children learn best when they can take responsibility for their actions by making amends and owning up to their (inappropriate) choice.

> Children learn best when they can take responsibility for their actions by making amends, rather than experiencing shaming punishment.

When Charlie makes a mess in the kitchen, he must clean it up before he can do anything else. He cannot watch his favorite TV show and *do it later*; he must make amends in the moment. If he refuses or has a tantrum, the parent must wait it out. Referring to the *rule book* will help the parent remain more neutral. Charlie may attempt to leave the kitchen without completing his chore. The parent must calmly redirect him to the mess and not allow him to leave the area until the job is done. For young children, it is appropriate to help them get started; for older children, your calm, patient, but emphatic insistence will get the message across. Charlie will eventually do his job as he will want to go back to play.

For children three and over, the time needed to get results will decrease dramatically if a parent consistently applies the consequence. It is inconsistency that keeps children violating the same rules over and over again. One day parents ignore, another they yell; another they clean up the mess themselves and another they take away a privilege.

Of course, in the real world, parents don't always have the time to follow through consistently. When these times inevitably occur, take care of the incident as neutrally as possible (i.e., clean up the mess yourself) and remember there will always be a next instance when you can help your child learn more effectively.

Notice that this approach eliminates yelling and screaming, and eliminates that deep sense of shame that a child feels when his parents get that angry. At the same time, the parents are able to teach a rule, and to have an agreed upon consequence that is logical for the violation. The child will feel some remorse and begin to think about a different course when faced with a similar situation in the future.

Once again, our theme is that conflicts are opportunities, not dangers to flee or quash.

TIME OUTS

for toddlers and even for some older children, time outs can be effective in getting the message across that a rule has been broken. The problem with time outs is that they do not teach the child any skills for behaving in a new, more appropriate way. The time out simply teaches that whatever he or she did is unacceptable.

In fact, time outs can actually reinforce inappropriate behavior. If parents find themselves having to hold their child in a chair or constantly bringing her back to the corner, the youngster is getting what she wants: attention (and physical attention at that) from her parent.

There are moments when a time out from the action is appropriate. When the child has pushed all the parent's buttons and the parent feels that he or she is going to *lose it*, or the child is simply unable to manage his body or words, then it is quite appropriate for the parent to tell the child he must go to a *cooling down* place. This differs from a classic time out because you do not set a time or indicate when the child can return to the situation. Choose a place where he can sit and maybe even look at some books. Tell the child, "You are having so much trouble managing your body you cannot be in the room with us; you can join us when you are ready to manage and then we can talk about what has happened." The child may run right back into the situation and resume his inappropriate behavior. If this happens, simply say, "*You thought you were ready, but I see you are not. You will need to go back until you are ready to be with us.*"

remember: this is *not* a punishment. It is recognition that your child is struggling with a feeling or a rule and you are empowering him by helping him become aware of his feelings, which will allow him to choose another course of behavior in the future.

INVERTED TIME OUTS

occasionally, a child has such a hard time managing that the parents must take more action. This child will not go to the cooling down place or keeps coming back and acting in an inappropriate manner. An effective technique to use with children two and a half and over is to say, "*I see that today you are having so much trouble managing that I will have to go into the other room until you think you can be with me without hurting (or yelling or throwing...).*"

This may be thought of as an inverted time out. Instead of the child being removed, the adults remove themselves and any other children that are with them. Simply go into any room that has a door and close it. Your child will most likely come running after you, pounding on the door. Re-open the door and say, *"I would love to be with you, but I cannot be with you when you are hitting (screaming, throwing things, etc.)."* That is because your attention and physical presence is what the child wants. You can help label the big feelings that are causing the scene: *"I know that you are mad because you wanted ice cream (want me to put the baby down, get off the phone, etc.), but you cannot act this way."* This allows for the acceptance of feelings (you are so mad, you cannot manage your body) while permitting the child to develop control over his emotions. The child learns what he has to do to get back in control and get you back and begins to internalize these important lessons.

W

Chapter Five

DISCIPLINE: SPECIFIC AGES AND SPECIAL SITUATIONS

"You may give them your love but not your thoughts,
for they have their own thoughts."
— Kahlil Gibran

OBSERVATIONS AT VARIOUS AGES

clearly, discipline techniques must vary according to the ages of the children. Understanding the developmental stages of children and how these stages impact behavior can help a parent gain some insight into their conduct.

INFANCY: THE SEEDS OF EXPECTATIONS

in the first months of a child's life, she really does get to dictate the rhythm of her days. But as your infant approaches the end of the first year and becomes mobile, you will be faced with the issue of how you are going to set limits. Your consistent reactions, tone of voice, and facial expressions will be the most effective tools you will have when beginning to teach your young toddler how to be safe. A child of one who dumps her toys on the floor is exploring materials in a most appropriate way and should not be stopped. However, even at this age, she can be shown how to put them away. You have no expectation of her doing this on her own. You are simply setting the seeds for future behavior. Reading your baby's signals will help you make appropriate choices for her. Some babies are very sensitive to crowds or noises or strangers. When in unfamiliar surroundings, the ability to read your child will help her cope and result in a more pleasant experience.

> Discipline in infancy is mainly setting the seeds of expectation for future behavior, a practice of the rules you consider most important.

Marcia was attending a birthday party with her five-year-old at one of those pizza places with characters in costumes and moving creatures coming out of the walls at the children. Marcia noticed that her 10-month-old, whom she was holding in her arms became agitated, fussing and twisting her body. Marcia realized that the din and confusion of this place was simply too much for her baby and spent the rest of the party outside in the parking lot. This mother missed out on the adult socialization, but she did what was necessary for her baby's comfort.

Learning to read your baby's signals takes time and patience; some babies make their feelings apparent while others are almost enigmatic. First time parents who have a child that is "hard to read" often feel that they don't know how to comfort their child and consequently feel incompetent. These feelings can lead to a parent who does not set boundaries and expectations. We encourage all parents to take the time and watch your infant with the purpose of learning to read their signals in your mind.

TODDLER YEARS:
THE POWER OF HUMAN CONSCIOUSNESS

do the "terrible twos" really exist? Most parents gird themselves for the onslaught of stubborn, unpredictable behavior that can be the hallmarks of this age. This stage, the "terrible twos," actually often begins around 18 months of age, and is the result of a rather extraordinary event, the emergence of your child's human consciousness.

> It is the development of consciousness at roughly 18 months of age that causes the onset of a period of strong surging emotions and tantrums

Surely newborns are aware of hunger, your presence, and myriad aspects of their world, but they are not conscious of them. They know when they are hungry and cry to eat, but they are not aware of that awareness. As a result, when the need is met, the young infant will simply be content, not consciously aware that although all is well, it could be better. **With consciousness, the situation changes radically, and forever.** Now a myriad of needs and desires are brought to our consciousness for consideration and reaction. Instead of simply liking a meal, we weigh it in our conscious minds and wonder how it could be better. The even, steady contentment of infancy gives way to how most of us spend our lives, with a series of surges of happiness alternating with sudden drops from disappointments, and an infinite array of hopes and dreams. Just as the first thing anyone learning to walk does is fall, so too the person learning to manage this flood of unmet desires and dreams is to be overwhelmed and to shut down. Tantrums are a collapse of the child's ability to manage all the competing feelings and desires that come with consciousness.

in a tantrum, the child has little control over the chaotic rush of feeling, and all we can do when this occurs is wait for the tantrum to pass, and for the more usual flow of feelings to resume. This is the meaning of tantrums and why they are so typical. The way a parent deals with them, however, can determine if the emergence of your child's consciousness will be a complex and emotionally powerful exploration, or will be terrible indeed.

> Tantrums are the collapse of the child's ability to manage all the competing feelings and desires that come with consciousness.

Many parents are distressed by tantrums. They are surprised to find that their once sweet tempered, easily distracted infant has turned into a demanding, illogical dictator. This transition is part of your child's social and emotional growth. As the toddler's conscious awareness increases, she realizes that her actions can change the world. It may appear that she is in an almost constant state of disequilibrium. If milk is good then milk with a straw may be better. A young child can make seemingly endless and sometimes irrational demands as she attempts to figure out how powerful she is at changing her environment. A child of this age is naturally becoming increasingly more independent from her caregivers and is becoming an individual quite separate from her parents.

Such a breaking away necessarily creates tension. The ambivalence between wanting to remain a baby and wanting to do things on her own is almost palpable at this time. The child is struggling with this issue of individuation; struggling with the enormous feelings of breaking away from the loving, care-giving parents and striking out on her own. Parents share this ambivalence as well. Certainly most parents look forward to the day when their child will not need them to attend to every physical and emotional need. Conversely, the loss of their baby's dependence on them can stir up some potent emotions. Parents who have difficulty allowing their baby to grow up and away from them hinder their child's overall development. Saying goodbye to the pacifier, bottle, diapers, or crib is as difficult for some parents as it is for the child. Parents may have low expectations in these areas for their child because they believe that it would be harmful, even traumatic, for a child to be helped to put away baby things and move to the next plateau. Consequently, children who are already ambivalent about this process get a response from their parent that undermines the growing up part and reinforces the "you are still a baby" part.

> *Ida, two months shy of her third birthday, used her pacifier 24 hours a day. In full time child care, she walked around the room with her "binky" in her mouth, rarely talking or interacting with the other children. Her favorite activity was sitting on the teacher's lap and having a book read to her. She showed little interest in the other children and, when not with one of the teachers, played by herself. Her child care providers tried for months to convince her parents that the pacifier seemed to be interfering with her use of language and social development. Mother was reluctant to give up the pacifier; she was not sure how her daughter would react to its loss because of the intense attachment. Finally, after much preparation (for both parent and child) the pacifier was not allowed in the school room.*
> *The teachers had expected some changes but were amazed at the difference no pacifier made. Ida began moving around the room more freely. She called all the children by name and actively sought them out as playmates. She was, in fact, downright chatty and proved to have a keen sense of humor. The removal of the pacifier had much more significance than just "unplugging" Ida. The parent's participation in helping Ida say goodbye to a remnant of babyhood gave her the message that she was indeed a big girl — and she began to act accordingly.*

biting is an issue that often comes up with toddlers. Biting is not atypical in children ages 10 months through two years. For younger toddlers, biting is often a natural outgrowth of their oral exploration of the world; for older toddlers it may be a response to a frustrating experience such as another invading their space or taking a toy. Biting is often used when children lack the language skills to make their needs known.

> *Jessica's son Todd was 20 months old. He was sitting on her lap during playgroup and suddenly turned and bit her, hard, on her shoulder. She laughed a bit and said*

to him, "Oh, Todd, you know biting hurts Mommy. Please don't do that anymore." All of this while still holding him and talking in a lilting, almost playful voice. Was it the presence of her friends that kept Jessica from using a voice that would get Todd's attention, or did she believe that since toddlers do still bite that discipline was uncalled for in this situation?

Biting is a situation that does not have to be tolerated — no matter what the age of your child. For the infant or toddler who bites: Put him down on the ground and firmly say "No, biting hurts." Wait a few moments before picking up the child again. This temporary removal of "you" is the most effective technique. Biting or hitting a child to show him how it feels simply teaches that biting and hitting is tolerated. For the older toddler, a similar technique can be used. Jessica might have removed Todd from her lap and said, "Ouch!! Biting hurts. You may not sit on my lap if you bite." When a child bites a peer, remove him from the situation with firm words and give attention to the victim. If the biter is able, let him help you get an ice pack to put on the injured child. After stopping the action you can add words that will help your child with an alternative: "I saw that you were mad that John took the train you were playing with. Next time say, 'No!'" You might even have him practice saying the words that will get him results without the biting.

THREES AND FOURS:
THE EMERGENCE OF SELF, THE ABILITY TO
UNDERSTAND COMPLEX ADULT CONVERSATION

as has been noted throughout this book, raising children inherently involves dealing with conflicts. Children are born to simultaneously resist and learn. Once again, a certain amount of conflict is expected and is a healthy sign of your child's development. However, at times, parents can inadvertently cause behavioral problems that could otherwise be avoided, or at least minimized. Many of these problems stem from the parents not understanding the new stage of development their child has entered. Understanding your child's world from her point of view may help you circumvent some of these issues.

as children enter the preschool years, their world begins to expand in many ways. They are now being introduced to other adults whom they must trust will care for them in their parent's absence. They must learn to delay gratification as they are now part of a larger group, and they must learn how to get along with a variety of different personalities — how to be part of a group dynamic. They are also becoming increasingly aware of the larger world around them.

> As children enter the preschool years, they often need to expand the number of adults they trust, and begin to adapt to being part of a group of children.

Aaron, aged three, says to his mom, " I don't want to die from cancer." Mom is stunned. No one is their family has recently died and no one they know has cancer. From where does Aaron's concern come? Aaron is a bright child who perhaps picked up bit of adult conversation or overheard a television or radio report.

Parents are often surprised at how much information children can pick up even if it is not aimed directly at them. Children become aware that people can get hurt or get sick and mommies and daddies cannot always prevent it from happening or make it better. This is a time of great fears for children. Monsters lurk under beds, night lights are essential, and children fear things that just a few months before they embraced. What can parents do to calm their fear? One of the most important things they can do is to carefully monitor and limit television and video watching.

young children easily blur the lines between reality and fantasy. Even movies that are supposedly made for children often contain themes and visual imagery that simply overwhelm young children. Classics like *The Wizard of Oz* are wonderful, but they are not for most preschoolers. Parents will claim that their child "loves" a certain video, which contains frightening material, and that the child "watches it over and over again" and, in fact, acts out character roles and even seems obsessed by it. Children who engage in this type of behavior are clearly trying to master a great fear by watching it again and again, trying to grasp what is real and what is not. Putting away these videos until the child is school-age is not easy but, despite protestations, your child will be relieved that you are protecting him from viewing these scary images.

THE SURPRISING ABILITY OF CHILDREN TO PICK UP INFORMATION: REFERENTIAL HEARING

most parents are aware that their child understands things even before she can coherently speak about them. Yet, many parents underestimate the ability of their child to pick up information from informal conversations and, consequently, expose her to information that causes behavior puzzles.

Lisa, age three, was simply unable to enter her preschool classroom without screaming and yelling. This was surprising because it was halfway through the year and she and her mother had apparently gone through a successful separation process in September. What was the cause for this intense behavior? Some conversations with the mother revealed that this mom had developed a particular dislike for one of the teachers. The director suggested that Lisa was picking up some "bad vibes" from the mom. Mom said that was impossible because she only talked about the teacher when Lisa was in the other room watching TV. She asserted that Lisa was not paying attention to her telephone calls to friends about the classroom situation. As an experiment, the director asked the mother to make some very positive comments about the teacher and, in fact, come into the room and do a special project with the teacher, even calling her a friend. Lisa watched this little drama playing out and said to her mother, "Why are you playing with Mrs. B? I thought you hated her." No wonder Lisa was afraid to enter her classroom. Her mother had made it very clear (although unknowingly) to her that her teacher was not a safe person. As your children reach the age of three and four, they are far more receptive to information than at age one or two, so exercise appropriate caution.

As your children reach the age of three and four, they are far more receptive to information than at age one or two, so exercise appropriate caution.

CHILDREN WITH SPECIAL NEEDS REQUIRE SPECIAL HELP

most parents are aware that some children are more compliant or easygoing by nature. There is no doubt that some children are more difficult to parent than others. These are the children for whom the normal developmental processes seem to be fraught with more struggle, more negativity, and more conflict than typically seen. There are many reasons for these difficulties and parents have to act as detectives as they attempt to figure out what is going on with their child and what tactics will be the most helpful. At times, it is simply a matter of adjusting the parenting style to a child whose temperament calls for more consistent boundary setting. For other children, these intense struggles signal a more serious issue. Children who have developmental delays, affective issues, or attention deficit problems often have behavioral difficulties as preschoolers. Parents who suspect that their child's development is not typical should consult with their pediatrician about these concerns. Enrolling your child in a quality preschool may also help parents determine how their child's behavior compares to other children the same age.

max's lack of connection.

In a "mom and me" class for two-year-olds, Helen observed that while the other children walked around playing with toys and engaging with the teachers, her son Max spent most of his time lying on the carpet rubbing his hand back and forth. Attempts by the teachers to interest him in the various activities met with limited success. The teachers were concerned about Max's lack of eye contact and general ability to be engaged in the classroom, and shared these concerns with his mom. Helen, who had noticed these things herself, used the teachers' comments to convince her husband and in-laws that an evaluation should be done. In fact, Max was found to have some delays and appropriate therapies were prescribed. This early intervention allowed Max to remain in the traditional preschool with the need for only minor adjustments.

SUMMARY

- Discipline is frequently viewed as the need to punish children for violations of rules. When viewed as such, parents feel trapped into choosing to be harsh, or to avoid being harsh becoming too lenient. Many feel that simply caring will resolve the dilemma by removing the need for discipline.

- A more accurate and powerful concept of discipline is the art of teaching your children important rules. These are rules that protect their safety, allow them to participate in their culture with friends and family, and allow them to participate outside the home at school and play.

- Children all have a strong desire to learn the rules their family and culture value most, and at the same time need to resist those rules to both strengthen their sense of self, and to learn how strongly each rule is truly valued.

key elements that will help you teach your children and apply the rules include:

- Effective language strategies

- Clarity of just what the rules are and what the consequences are for breaking them.

- Agreement between the parents on which rules are the most important.

- An explicit listing of those rules so the child knows what they are.

- Clear consequences that occur consistently when the rules are broken.

- Establishing the rule as the reason for the consequence, allowing the parent to remove himself directly from the situation.

- Ensuring that teaching remains the central concern of discipline. Consequences, when called for, are part of the teaching process, and should not be relied on as the key aspect of discipline.

- Repetition is a key aspect of teaching at all ages, and should be expected and tolerated patiently

- Knowledge of aspects or qualities of certain ages and situations will help refine your ability to guide or teach your children.

- Experiencing conflicts when teaching our children the rules is perhaps the most universal aspect of this area of teaching, and is necessary for the child's normal development.

- Finally, some developmental, affective, cognitive and/or attention issues may make learning rules more difficult than it should be, and professional help may be required to help the family effectively teach or discipline.

W

Chapter Six

TOILET MASTERY

"The struggle alone pleases us, not the victory."
— Blaise Pascal

for many parents, the issue of potty training is one that causes enormous anxiety and concern. Parents are both fearful of causing their child permanent psychological harm and of having a child who will not be ready to attend preschool or otherwise be in synch with his peers. The parent in the twenty-first century is likely to read magazine articles and books about the subject. They may consult their pediatrician or listen to their friends. Most often, they do *not* listen to their own parents' admonitions that they are missing the boat and do not care about the stories of their own potty success at 18 months. Most sources seem to be telling parents that there is really nothing they can do about this process — that the child must decide on her own to use the potty and, by waiting it out, success is assured. Pediatricians guarantee that no child ever walked down the aisle in diapers and television ads confirm the idea that it is acceptable for even older children to still wear (the brand new larger sized) diapers.

> Current guidance on toilet training emphasizes how little a parent can or should do.

Nagging in the back of many parents' minds, however, is the thought that somehow there *is* something that they should be doing to encourage their child. After all, up to this point most children have been weaned from the bottle or breast, given up their pacifier, or even moved to a big bed. All parents know that some children make these transitions with ease while others may struggle over each new hurdle. They have experienced the need for the parents to take a stand, on some issue, to help their child move through a developmental stage. Why, then, for this all-important process are parents advised to take a back seat?

One reason may be a backlash against the strict method of a generation or two ago. Many psychoanalytic approaches claimed that many adult neuroses could be traced to harsh toilet training. The expression "He's so anal" refers to a compulsive, overly neat person who presumably had a mother who spanked him when he dirtied himself. So ingrained is the idea that parents can harm their child by too early or too harsh toilet training that many parents become paralyzed and do nothing at all to aid their child in the toileting process. After all, if there is no parental direction, there can be no parent foul up. Parents often seem to lack the confidence to go ahead and start the process even if their child is showing readiness. Laura, mother of two, writes:

> **Most parents appropriately feel that they should be able to offer some guidance to help their child toilet train, and that sense is correct.**

I think there is a lot of pressure when you see kids the same age as your child trained or not trained. I have friends with kids older than Isabel that haven't even started. I don't talk about it with them because I'm afraid they'll think I'm pushing Isabel. Then you have people who think I'm not doing enough. It's difficult to feel confident in yourself.

pediatricians add to parents' ambivalence by making vague comments about "waiting until the child is ready" or by giving advice with no follow up. Sarah, mother of Kyle, age two and a half, states: "*My pediatrician said that when the child is ready it will happen and that no external pressure will change that.*"

Similarly, Susan's doctor told her that:

"when they are ready they will do it — don't worry about the age of the child." The trouble is that my daughter can't go to preschool and I'm expecting a second child in May. I also worry about whether she will ever be ready or that she is ready and I am missing the signals.

Mara's doctor told her to:

"put the child on the potty every day for five minutes after lunch." That was it!

Betsy, mother of two boys, ages one and three, was told to:

"buy a big toy and when 10 stickers were placed on the toy he would receive the toy."

None of these mothers found the advice helpful or complete enough to really help them understand the process. However, the simplistic advice made them feel that they were doing something wrong and seemed to stop the process in its tracks. Most parents would like a few more guidelines, not only about the "how to's" but also on the emotional investment that this step requires. Betsy writes:

I think next to walking and talking that this may be the most monumental event that occurs for the child and the parents in the first three years of life. The ambivalence and anxiousness in the parents can create a very explosive situation in the home. The books and the pediatricians tend to gloss over this point. I think it would be better if pediatricians could mention this point to parents before they get started so they know this is a normal part of the process.

> When guidance is offered, it often is too simple and incomplete, making parent and child both feel badly when it does not work

For some parents, the natural struggles of a toddler learning how to master his or her body is something they try to avoid. Pat shares:

I am not looking forward to starting. I feel it is not going to be positive and we are going to have a fight on our hands.

Instead of making use of the struggle that must precede mastery, parents fear this struggle and lower their expectations for the child. There is an overpowering urge for some parents to clear the child's developmental pathway of any stumbling blocks. Not only is this an impossible task, it is also risky. Children need the experience of dealing with these small struggles and frustrations to give them the skills to deal with larger issues that will inevitably come their way as they grow older. Parents do a child no favor by keeping him away from potentially difficult situations, for they also keep him from the splendid feeling that comes from a job well done. The look on an infant's face when she takes her first step or the elation a six-year-old feels when he rides his two-wheeler for the first time are the feelings of mastery that most everyone agrees are essential for healthy growth. Yet, by delaying toilet teaching, parents routinely deny their children the grown-up feeling of being in charge of their bodies. Certainly, being responsible for one's own body must be firmly in place before other kinds of mastery can occur.

When both parents work outside the home, toilet mastery is sometimes delayed. Often, caregivers or child care centers are not willing to put up with the mess that often accompanies the child's learning. At times, caregivers and parents are at odds about the timing and procedures. This can confuse the child and can certainly elongate the process. Additionally, parents who are not with their child for much of the day may be reluctant to make demands on him during their limited time together. Betsy adds:

> *My babysitter told me that she had too many children to watch to help Eli with cleaning up. She wanted him in diapers or pull ups until he was trained — but how could I train him if he was always in diapers?*

For some families, the change from diapers to *big boy pants* represents the loss of the *baby*. Some parents unconsciously sabotage the process because it means a kind of letting go of the child. Mary writes:

> *This is stressful because it is visible proof of the child's growing independence. It's one of many separations of parents and children for a child to master the potty, and the letting go part for parents is difficult.*

Although most of us look forward to the day when our child is free from diapers, this transition can be tinged with a sense of loss. For parents, the loss may be transitory but for the child the loss of his diapers can underscore his feelings of ambivalence. Ambivalence is the hallmark of the toddler. One day he wants to be a "big boy" and the next he wants to be a baby. One of the "terrible" things about twos is the inconsistency of their responses. Johnny won't let you dress him on Tuesday but on Wednesday, he lays there helpless, crying for you to help him. The same child, who won't keep by your side at the mall, will cling to you at a gathering of family members.

Ambivalence is the hallmark of the toddler, and should not discourage parent or child from making progress

Two-year-olds are in the process of figuring out where they end and you begin. They are individuating and separating themselves from their parents and this process causes many conflicting feelings. The urges to be both a grown-up girl and a baby, co-existing at one time, are bound to cause some contradictory responses.

paula uses the potty a few times a week but not consistently. David uses the potty for the sitter but never at home with Mom and Dad. Terry hasn't had an accident for a week, but suddenly is starting to wet his pants again. Parents often interpret these lapses as signs that the child is not ready to continue. Pediatricians often advise going back into diapers or stopping the process.

> *When I told my doctor that Sara stopped using the*

potty after several successful days and was asking for her diapers again, she told me to go ahead and give them back to her. She told me not to "stress her out" and that I should do nothing until she asked for her panties again.

The problem with this approach is that it reinforces the *baby* in the child and does not support the grown-up feeling. Instead, parents can imagine that their child is engaged in a tug-of-war with the *baby* on one side and the *big girl* on the other. On the days that the process is going smoothly, the *big girl* is winning; on less successful days, the *baby* is pulling harder. Parents must always take the side of the rope that the *big girl* is on if they want to let their child know that they are confident that she can do the very grown-up job of caring for her own body.

Parents receive so much conflicting advice from *their* parents, doctors, friends, and books that they are often overwhelmed by the prospect of getting started with their child. While realizing the uniqueness of each child and each family situation, there are specific steps that parents can use when helping their child master the toileting process.

HOW TO START

from the very start of your child's life, you can begin the mastery process by correctly labeling body parts and their bodily excretions. Around 18 months, parents can buy small potties that sit securely on the floor. At this stage, you can occasionally empty diapers into the pot. Your child will show some curiosity about the potty. Tell her this is where she will soon put all her pee and poops and allow her to sit on it whenever she wants. Right before bath time is a good opportunity for your child to get used to sitting on the potty without clothing. At this point, you have no expectations of your child actually producing anything on the potty. You are simply laying the groundwork. Setting the stage, so to speak.

IS MY CHILD READY?

by the time most children are 18 months old, they are physically capable of using the toilet. In some cultures, children under a year are routinely continent. Many parents underestimate their child's ability to be continent and interpret accidents as a lack of readiness rather than part of the mastery struggle.

Ellen, mother of Allan, age two years and nine months, said:

When Allan was outside playing naked in the wading pool he had no accidents. Suddenly he asked for his diaper. We put it on and he had a bowel movement. I was so surprised — I thought he had no idea when he had to urinate or have a B.M.

In the United States, some parents would not consider trying to introduce their child to the potty before his or her second birthday. Early potty training has become associated with harsh parental intervention and a host of psychological difficulties. Fear of not wanting to "push" their child often prevents parents from reading his or her readiness signals. It is a rare child who wakes up one morning and tells his parents that he wants to put away his diapers and use the potty from now on! Almost all children will need their parents' support and guidance during this important process.

There are many signs that your child is beginning to think about using the potty. You may notice that every time she is about to have a bowel movement, she goes into the corner and "does her business." Another child may show curiosity about the process by wanting to watch others or sitting on the potty fully clothed. Another child may show an interest in lining up his toys or putting them away in their proper spot, which indicates an understanding that everything has its place. Some children get into an "I want to do it myself" phase. They want to attempt to dress themselves, pour their own juice, buckle their car seats and so on. These actions should be encouraged. They are sure signs that your child is excited about his growing independence. If your child is reluctant to take on these new responsibilities, she should be gently but consistently helped to perform them.

The heart of this matter is often a seesaw between independence and dependence

This seesaw between independence and dependence is really at the heart of this matter. The actual product of getting the pee and poop into the potty is really just a by-product of the larger mastery process that the child goes through to achieve the goal. The process becomes part of the child as much as the ability to use the toilet. A child who learns that she can manage a frustrating situation and learn to make positive choices will be able to apply that same way of thinking to future struggles and problems.

FIRST STEPS

some time between 20 and 30 months, you may feel that the time is right for you and your child to begin the journey toward bodily independence. Besides your child's physical and psychological readiness, you must feel ready too. Try to choose a time when work or life schedules are less hectic. A new baby, a new house, or a family illness may interfere with your family's ability to cope with the inevitable stresses of starting this process. If you work, try to pick a weekend where you can take off an extra day or two to get your child started. Once you have decided to embark on the process, there are some specific steps you and your child can do.

• **start reading books that introduce the topic to your child.** There are a proliferation of books and videos on potty training. Any will do but two that are particularly useful are *Going to the Potty* by Fred Rogers (MisterRogers) and *No More Diapers!* by Joae Graham Brooks, M.D.

• **a few days before you are ready to start, take your child on a field trip to the shopping mall and purchase 12 to 18 pairs of training pants.** Training pants are cotton underwear that are considerably thicker than regular underpants. Parents often ask if *pull ups* should be used. Pull ups can be used for nap time or nighttime, so children can maintain some independence. However, during the day, they act and feel like more like diapers than underpants. At the time of this purchase, allow your child to pick out some grown-up underwear. There are many fancy pants that come with different designs and in different colors that should appeal to your child. Tell your child that these grown-up pants will be worn when he can keep his training pants clean and dry. The real underwear is a natural reward — a logical consequence of consistent use of the potty.

• **rearrange your child's room so that his training pants are easily accessible to him.** The changing table should be put away or, at least, given another purpose (such as holding toys or the new underwear). Diapers might be put on a closet shelf to be used only for nighttime. In other words, you are helping your child see that something is changing. Remind him that he will soon be wearing his big boy pants instead of his diapers.

- **on the morning of the first day, take off your child's diaper and remind him that "Today is the day you get to wear your big boy pants, all day!"** Most children will be excited about putting on the pants. However, occasionally, a child is so attuned to the loss of the diaper that he refuses. In this case, it is your job to remain neutral but firm about what is expected. Tell your child, *"I see you really want to wear your diaper now, but Mom and Dad know you are ready to wear big boy pants."* This is a very empowering, *you-can-do-it* message. Even so, your child may become upset and even cry for his diaper. At this junction, you must be clear in your resolve to help your child with this initial struggle. If you give him back his diaper, you are in essence telling him that he is *not* ready. On the other hand, if you permit him his feelings without participating in the struggle with him, you allow your child to take a major step toward being more grown-up. Eventually, your child will want to leave his room and will put on his underpants (with or without your help).

- **once your child is wearing his training pants, tell him that he is the boss of his pee and poop (you may use any words that feel comfortable for your family) and that training pants are for keeping clean and dry.** Let him know that when he feels like he has to go, he can use the potty on his own or ask you to help him. He can use the big potty or the one that sits on the floor. In other words, you are giving him some choices but are making the expectations clear. Some parents allow their child to wear just training pants and a shirt while in the house. Some children will refrain from going on the floor if naked. While this tactic may work, the child still needs to learn how to keep his pants dry.

- **soon after you make these positive pronouncements, expect to see your child walking around awkwardly because his pants are no longer clean or dry.** They are called training pants because accidents are to be expected. It is the only way your child can understand the consequences of *not* using the potty. It is your reaction that is key here. You might start with an observation. *"I see your pants are wet (have a poop in them). Remember big boy pants are for keeping clean and dry. You are the boss of your body and when you poop (or pee) in them, it is your job to clean yourself up."*

- **expecting the child to clean up his messes is the step with which many parents have the most trouble.** The underlying theme of this method is that the child must take responsibility for his or her own body. When a child is being trained, it is the parent who is responsible for directing the action and who can take credit for successes and failures. This method is based on mastery where the child directs the actions, takes responsibility, and can take credit for his own successes and feel the consequences of any failures.

• **the clean up procedure takes some time, which is why a more relaxed family schedule is helpful before embarking on the process.** Some children will immediately inform their parents of an accident. Others will try to keep it hidden. As soon as you notice, use words to remind him of your expectations and then help him to the bathroom for the clean up. Do *not* lay your child down on the floor or the changing table to change him. Tell him, *"Your pants are not clean and it is your job to clean up."* Ask him to pull his pants down. At this point, some children will look at you with complete bewilderment. After all, for two and a half or three years, this has been *your* job and now you are expecting him to do it. Expect some children to resist this suggestion. Do not make this a battle ground. You might tell your child, *"I see you do not want to do this now, but you are the boss of your body and it is your job to clean up. Here, I will help you get started."* At this point, a parent can place his or her hands over the child's and help him pull down his pants. Have a bucket or an old diaper pail available for the soiled pants. Give your child a sponge or paper towels to clean up any messes on the floor. Give him plenty of toilet paper to wipe himself. Flushable wipes are great for this purpose. Be sure to show girls how to wipe from back to front to avoid infection. If your child has had a messy B.M., the chances are that you will have to assist him, but allow him to start the process. Generally, the less you do and the more your child does, the quicker the process will be.

• **you repeat this process with as much consistency as you can throughout the learning period.** At times, commitments will make it impossible for you to allow the child as much time as he needs for clean up. Do not worry when you cannot follow the procedure as closely as you would like. As long as your overall expectations are clear, your child will get the message: this is his body and he is the one in charge of it! What a wonderful feeling for your toddler. You have empowered your child in an appropriate, positive way.

• **when your child does use the potty, praise him in a way that tells him he must feel good about what he has done.** Instead of, *"What a good boy you are"* or *"Daddy is so proud,"* you might say, *"How proud you must feel — what a big boy feeling! Your pants are clean and* *dry."* Since we have given the child the responsibility for this process, we must also give him the kudos that go with a job well done. Parents often have many questions about the process in general. Here are some common areas of concern:

IMPORTANT QUESTIONS AND ANSWERS

what if my child just refuses to clean up?

It is hard not to feel angry with a child who will not comply. If your child will not accompany you to the bathroom for a clean up you might say, *"I see you don't want to clean up right now, but you are the one who peed in his pants and it is your job to clean up. I think you will feel better about yourself if you walk to the bathroom holding my hand, but if you can't I will pick you up and carry you there. The bathroom is the place to clean up pee and poop."*

ok, he's in the bathroom, now what?

Gently but firmly remind your child that this is his job now. If he is really upset you may have to wait a few minutes until he calms down to proceed. It is at this point that many parents worry that they are doing something wrong. After all, if they were doing it right, would their child be so upset? Remember that these protestations are the external manifestation of your child's inner struggle to leave the baby behind and become grown-up. For some children this struggle is intense. It is, in fact, particularly with this type of child that you want to keep your expectations firm and clear. Your child is in turmoil but you must be a rock, guiding him and supporting him through this major developmental milestone.

my child cleans up too readily — he seems to love it, so this part is not working!
Remember, the clean up is *not* a punishment. It is the logical consequence of messy pants. It is meant to give your child control over the situation and help him accept responsibility for his bodily functions.

what do I do when we go out for the day? Can I put him back into diapers?
When a child goes in and out of diapers he gets a very mixed message from his parents. A helpful hint is to put a pair of plastic pants over the training pants to minimize the by-products of accidents. Use these sparingly, when you really cannot deal with an accident. Simply explain to your child that you know it is hard to remember to use the potty all the time when you are out of the house.

should I put my child on the potty every 20 or 30 minutes? My neighbor told me this was the method that worked for her. When parents take the initiative for placing their child on the potty, they are taking responsibility for the process. Suggesting that your child use the potty at logical times during the day makes more sense. Right before a car ride, when you are washing your hands before lunch, or at bath time are times that often meet with less resistance. However, if you say, *"We are going to the park now. Let's try to use the potty"* and you are met with a resounding *"NO,"* back down immediately. You might say, *"I see you are not ready to use the potty right now. I will show you where the toilet is when we get to where we are going. Remember it is your job to keep your pants clean and dry."*

my doctor suggested that I use stickers or a piece of candy for each success. Is that helpful? Most parents report that stickers have a short lived effect on their child's behavior. Once the novelty has worn off, the child often goes back to wetting his pants. Experience shows us that stickers and other external rewards work best in situations where a child (often an older one) has become so stuck in his refusal to use the toilet that the prize offers a way out with a bit of face-saving. Food items are so closely related to the whole elimination process that they often confuse the entire process. The idea of mastery is that the child learns to work primarily for internal rather than external rewards.

my daughter wants me to sit and read to her while she's on the potty. I don't mind, but she can sit for a half hour without going and then gets up and wets her pants a minute later. Does this mean she is not ready to begin the process? On the contrary, this tells you that your daughter has amazing control. We challenge you to sit on the toilet for a half hour without going! As long as you read to her, you are giving her your undivided attention. She has very little motivation to use the potty, because her success will mark your leaving to attend to other things. When she wets herself immediately after sitting for so long, you must attend to her some more. Allow a child to bring whatever she likes into the bathroom to amuse *herself.* You can be close by, reading a newspaper, folding laundry, etc., but this is her job and hers alone.

my child care program (caregiver) can't tolerate the accidents. What do I do? This is a major issue for many parents. One solution is to pick a time when you are on vacation so you can have the primary involvement. Another is to put plastic pants over the training pants during child care hours. If your caregiver absolutely refuses to have a child in training pants, you may have to use pull ups during these hours. While this can slow the process considerably, your child can still learn what *your* expectations are.

is it helpful for my child to see me or my spouse use the toilet? There are some difficulties in allowing your child to view you in the bathroom. After all, adult genitalia look quite different from a child's and some children become frightened or confused about these differences. Watching children of similar ages and the same sex is usually OK for most children. In fact, in a child care situation, knowing that others are using the toilet can be a powerful motivation for some children. A note of caution — mothers should be especially careful about allowing their children to see them in the bathroom while they are menstruating. To a young child, bloody pads and tampons look like there has been an injury. Your toddler has enough concerns about the workings of his body without this added visual confusion.

it has been one week with almost no successes. Is this a sign that I should just stop and go back to diapers? Although one week of messy pants can seem like a lifetime, if you previously felt that this was the right time you will probably want to persevere. Although most parents cannot remember learning to use the potty, they do remember learning to ride a two wheeler bicycle. Imagine if your father put you right back on your tricycle after a few falls from your bike. Mastery takes time and the message we want to give our child is that we have confidence in his ability to get the job done, no matter how frustrating and difficult it seems.

how long should this process take? While there are no guarantees, most children whose parents help them embark upon this process usually take from two to four weeks to get to the point where they are using the potty almost all the time. Of course, this varies widely. The child who is deeply feeling the loss of his diapers and the loss of contact with the parent that diaper-changing brings may take longer. The child who is more excited about the big boy pants and the independence may take only a few days to master this.

are there any times when a parent should seek professional help? Absolutely. Occasionally, a child gets "stuck" in a certain developmental stage and he and his parents may need outside help to move on to the next level. At times, it is the parent who finds him or herself so stirred up about this process that he or she needs to seek support to better understand why his or her feelings are interfering with the ability to support the child.

should I withhold treats if my child does not use the potty? For instance, tell him there will no dessert if he poops in his pants. Logical consequences work best to help children understand what is expected. There is no logical connection between withholding dessert and pooping in pants. However, if your child is outside at the park and has an accident, taking him home to clean up (and consequently missing play time) is connected directly to his actions. At home, the TV gets switched off, the lunch gets left, the cake batter is not stirred when you child must leave these activities to take care of his body. Soon, he will understand that using the potty is quicker, neater, and makes him feel good about himself!

my son uses the potty to pee but makes all his bowel movements in his pants. What should I do? It is not uncommon that children are a bit more reluctant to put their B.M.s in the potty. After all, a B.M. really looks like something important and many children only do it once a day. You can start by telling your child that a B.M is just the food that we eat that we don't need to make us grow bigger and that we make more every day. There are some books on this subject that are written for the young child. Some children feel insecure with their feet dangling from a big toilet so even if your child likes to pee in the regular toilet, you may want to provide a low potty where a child can sit with feet firmly planted on the ground. Some children like to put toilet paper or a paper towel over their potty before they have a B.M so they feel something on their buttocks. Some parents have found it helpful for their child to put paper or newspaper *next* to the potty so their child can eliminate on the floor and then put it in the toilet. Although no one is suggesting that your child is like a cocker spaniel, this method works especially well for children who seem to have an aversion to sitting on the potty.

my child won't have a B.M at all and is becoming constipated. Some children do not want to soil themselves but are still conflicted about using the potty. Enemas and suppositories are strongly cautioned against. These are invasive procedures which take away control from the child and can feel like a real attack on the child's body. Instead, consult your doctor about stool softeners that can be put in juice that will help your child stay regular. Some children will ask for their diaper to have a B.M. This is a slippery slope. It is not uncommon for children as old as six to still demand a diaper to have a bowel movement when this procedure was allowed from the beginning. However, if your child has not gone for several days you may choose to do this. Some parents put a diaper on when the child sleeps and the child will have a B.M during that time. Most times, this struggle is short lived. However, if your child is consistently constipated over several months, you may want to seek advice from a therapist who specializes in child development.

why use this method at all? Isn't it true that no one does walk down the aisle in diapers? Although almost all children will eventually figure out how to use the toilet, many parents appreciate a plan that helps them and their child feel in control. They understand that a thoughtful process where expectations and goals are clear helps a child not just master the potty but in other areas of life as well. After all, this is the first major thing you have asked of your child where you did not have the ultimate control. Parents can throw away a pacifier or the bottle but they cannot use the toilet for their child. This process allows a child to learn that he can accomplish a goal even if the road to such an accomplishment is filled with some frustration and struggle. As your child proceeds in life, he will be faced with tasks that are difficult and even discouraging. A child whose parent helps him understand how to master such situations acquires a skill which he can continually develop as he is faced with the inevitable challenges of life.

STORIES FROM THE EDGE (OF THE POTTY, THAT IS)

sometimes it is helpful for parents to read about how this process went for other families. Here are some actual stories from the front that reflect some typical and unique situations.

SAM'S STORY

sam was a very bright boy of three who was in full time child care when his parents helped him master the potty. To their delight, within two weeks he was using the potty at home for both pee and poop, 100 percent of the time. However, he absolutely refused to use the potty at school. This, of course, caused some difficulty for a child who was away for up to 10 hours a day. Naturally, there were daily accidents. The child care followed the parents' lead, letting Sam clean up his messes and he often missed special class times because he was busy in the bathroom. This went on for months with absolutely no successes. The parents sought help from a therapist who supported both the child care center and the parents through this trying time. Sam continued to use the potty appropriately at home and outside of the home when he was with his parents. After an extended period of accidents at school and after several months of therapy there was a breakthrough. Sam was encouraged to sit on the potty by his teacher and although he said he was finished, he made no attempt to get off the toilet. After many minutes, with tears streaming down his face, Sam used the toilet for the first time at school. He was four and a half years old. The parents told the child care that that night Sam finally revealed his worry. He thought that if he used the potty at school that he would have to sleep there and that his parents would not pick him up. Clearly, neither the school nor his parents had ever said such a thing, but the magical thinking of a preschooler had kept Sam stuck in this untenable situation. Here is a situation where outside help combined with parents and caregivers acting in partnership helped a little boy through a difficult time.

LISA'S STORY

two and a half-year-old Lisa mastered peeing in the potty after just a few days. Pooping was another matter. Mom was asking Lisa to do her own clean up, but Lisa was pretty adamant that this was not her job. Her mom wanted to know just how much she should demand of her since she was resisting so. Mom was advised to be kind but firm in her expectations about cleaning up. Within a few days, Mom reported that after one accident, Lisa looked up at her with tears in her eyes and said, "OK, I'll clean up my poop, but will you still make me my lunch?" Clearly, Lisa somehow felt that if she were the one completely in charge of her body that her mother would cease to perform other parental duties.

This is a common concern of young children. Parents might want to tell their children during a quiet time together that even big girls and boys who use the toilet all by themselves still have their mommies and daddies to feed them, put them to bed, and take care of them in so many other ways.

MAY AND ALICE'S STORY

may and alice are identical twins whose parents helped them embark upon this process when they were about two and a half. Alice seemed to pick up on what was expected immediately, while May appeared to show no interest. After some time, with Alice becoming completely continent and May still refusing, Mom asked May why she wouldn't use the potty. Giving her mother an incredulous look, May said, "Why should I? Alice uses it."

Twins do present special issues. Parents have to decide if they will start both children at the same moment or do them one at a time. Usually, starting together gives both children the message that they are capable, but twins do not always develop at the same rate and each family must make the choice that feels right for them.

ESTHER'S STORY

esther was about 20 months old when she began to ask to use the potty. Her mother complied with her wishes, taking off her diaper and putting her on the toilet when she asked. In a very short while, it was apparent that Esther kept her diaper clean and dry all the time. Esther's mother wanted to know if she should put her in pants. It seemed to fly in the face of logic to put such a young child in underpants. If she stopped using the toilet, would she have to put her back in diapers? Esther's mom bided her time for a few more weeks until she felt that the successes were not flukes. Esther wore her big girl pants with pride and never looked back.

Esther was a child who was invested in being grown-up. Although not typical, some children *do* seem to learn to use the toilet on their own with little or no parental intervention. These are the children who are always brought up as examples in pediatrician's offices and at playgroups. It is wise to remember that most children do not typically give up their diapers with such ease.

JACOB'S STORY

jacob was a gifted child approaching five who had developed a unique scenario while having a bowel movement. He would undress completely, have the B.M., and then call for his mother to come and wipe him. This had been their routine since he began regularly using the toilet at age three. His mother, realizing that she would not be available for this chore once he began kindergarten, sought advice. Her advisor simply told her to tell Jacob that she was no longer in charge of wiping him, and that it was his body and he needed to take care of himself. After some protests, Jacob complied. Not only did he wipe himself but he also ended the ritual of undressing before toileting.

Although almost five, Jacob was still trying to drag his parent into the toileting process. Both mother and child had allowed this remnant from the past to bind them together. Jacob had truly struggled with his initial toilet mastery and his mother still feared a regression in this area. Her ability to encourage Jacob to take complete charge of his body was needed for the process to be completely his. This same mother made an insightful comment a few years later as her second son, Sammy, breezed through the same process that had been such a struggle for his older brother. She said, "Sammy was enamored by the idea of being a *big boy*, while Jacob seemed to be in touch only with what the loss of the diapers meant." Each child will approach this process differently and we need to respect these differences.

SALLY'S STORY

sally was the second of two girls and had a rather unremarkable history when it came to learning to urinate in the potty. Having her bowel movements was another story. She would not use the toilet and insisted on having a diaper when she needed to defecate. Sally was approaching four and her mother was getting a bit tired of this routine. Sally's mother had to carry around a diaper at all times and was somewhat embarrassed by Sally's demand for it when she had to have a B.M. She also felt that Sally was somewhat humiliated by this action as children were noticing and beginning to make fun of her. Sally's mother decided to become proactive. She told Sally that when the diapers in the package were used up, they were not going to buy any more. Sally became distressed the day there were no more diapers and her mother's resolve began to wear thin as Sally begged for the diaper with real tears in her eyes. Although there was some anger and some soiled pants, within a few days, Sally was using the toilet for her B.Ms.

Sally's enhanced self-esteem more than made up for any temporary disappointment or indignation she felt when she no longer had her diaper. Sally's need for a diaper for her B.M allowed her to pull her mother into her struggle. The mother's ability to finally stand apart and encourage her child to use her own resources not only helped the immediate situation but laid the groundwork for future problem solving.

JERRY'S STORY

jerry was the youngest of three children and had mastered toileting at about the age of two and a half. About two or three times a month, however, Jerry would poop in his pants. Eventually, his mother realized that these *accidents* always occurred when he was mad at his parents. After one of these episodes, while Jerry was cleaning himself up, his mother said plainly to him, *"Jerry, you have big boy words to tell me you're mad. You do not need to poop in your pants to tell me you're angry."* Jerry looked up at his mother, soiled washcloth in hand and said, *"This is disgusting. I'm never going to do this again."* And he didn't.

Children will often use toileting accidents as a signal that they are upset or concerned. When soiling or wetting go on for extended periods or, especially if a child is clean and dry for a considerable period and *then* begins having accidents, there is often some other issue at play beyond just the toilet mastery. Observation of when accidents occur and the child's general behavior may give you some clues as to what these types of accidents are really about.

SUMMARY

toilet mastery, like the issues of sleeping, feeding, and discipline, is frequently experienced as its own special struggle. And as with each of these other situations, the conflicts created by toilet training often are perceived as unique and very difficult to manage. We present a perspective that hopefully will allow you to consider toilet training in a new light. We hope you can now see it as similar to other conflicts we experience with our children, an opportunity for learning together rather than as a fight.

    With regard to toilet mastery itself, we hope you can now appreciate that the key aspect of the process is your child taking over a responsibility from you. This assumption of responsibility is precisely what they seek and what they avoid, and what we as parents must teach.

W

Chapter Seven
CHILD CARE DILEMMAS

"Who has not felt so sadly sweet
The dream of home, the dream of home?"
— Thomas Moore

this chapter is not about *finding* a good child care solution for your young child. Cost, cleanliness, staff ratios, location and the like are the deciding factors for every family where both parents work outside of the home. This chapter will hopefully give some guidelines to parents *after* they have made their choice. Finding the right place is just the first step — now the really hard work is about to begin.

When parents put their child in the care of another, they are faced with a paradoxical situation: on one hand, they want their child to be cared for by a person who will really love and nurture her; on the other hand, they must deal with the fact that their child will form a close attachment with someone other than themselves. Eva, a mother of a preschooler, described it this way: "I prefer to get an au pair (instead of a nanny) whom I know will stay no more than a year. That way my son won't get 'too attached' to another person." Unfortunately, Eva did not understand that to successfully leave your child, a parent must permit and actually promote the special attachment between caregiver and child. What does it mean to "successfully leave" your child? After all, once you are comfortable with your care situation, how hard can it be to leave? Very. We have spoken about the ambivalence that toddlers and preschoolers have about toileting but ambivalence is no stranger to grown ups either. Most parents have some mixed feelings about leaving their youngsters, but the way that they deal with these feelings can make a tremendous difference in their children's behavior.

> Most parents have some mixed feelings about leaving their youngsters, but the way that they deal with these feelings can make a tremendous difference in their children's behavior.

THE LONG GOODBYE

parents are often surprised when their infant becomes a toddler and the relatively easy morning separation now becomes a major struggle. Developmentally, the 18 month and older child can now keep images in his mind and can anticipate the coming separation and the concurrent feelings that attend it. This is another aspect of the emergence of consciousness described in our discussion on discipline. Children will often employ delaying tactics in the home which can escalate into a full blown expression of crying and clinging at the center. Dad needs to get to work but yet he feels that his distressed child needs his attention. He begins to give into demands that make him angry at himself and at his child.

> The appearance of separation anxiety can often catch parents by surprise.

GORDON AND ADAM'S STORY, PART ONE:

gordon took his son to child care every morning while his wife picked up the child in the evening. Many times, Gordon thought he was getting the raw end of the deal. Gordon dreaded the alarm clock because it would signal the start of one struggle after another with his son, Adam. First, there was the complete inability to dress himself, although at three and a half Adam could accomplish most of this on his own; then it was a fight over what to have for breakfast. More often than not, oatmeal (Mom's suggestion) was replaced by a sweet pastry; then there was the ceremony of *putting on the jacket*. Either the jacket was refused or *it feels too tight* or it could not be found (Adam was able to find some pretty good hiding places). By the time the duo was in the car tensions were high as they both anticipated Round Two. At the center, Adam started his routine. He seemed incapable of hanging up his jacket and backpack (although his teachers reported that he could do all of these things during the school day). Adam would need his dad to do a puzzle and read a book with him. However, as Dad would finish one activity Adam would beg for *just one more*. Dad tried to be firm but Adam looked so disconsolate that he would give in if his schedule allowed.

Once Dad really left the room, Adam would run to the door and yell after him, *"You didn't kiss me goodbye!"* and begin to cry. Dad would return, looking grim, reminding him that he did indeed kiss him and the routine would have to start all over. Of course, Dad does finally get out but is left with the unsettling feeling that Adam's unhappiness will cause some permanent damage to his emotional development. Adam does not feel much better. He succeeded in temporarily getting his dad to stay and got some satisfaction from making his dad look so unhappy and worried, but he is also confused and sad because no one is taking control of a situation that, although full of emotion, is quite manageable.

A version of this scenario is played out in countless child care centers and homes throughout the country. And yet, some children and parents seem to manage a pleasant and even productive morning routine. It is likely that these are parents who have come to grips with their own ambivalent feelings about child care and are therefore able to help their offspring with their own feelings. A dad who allows himself to miss his son and, in turn, *allows his son to miss him* is on his way to a smoother transition from parent to caregiver.

> A dad who allows himself to miss his son and, in turn, *allows his son to miss him,* is on his way to a smoother transition from parent to caregiver.

GORDON AND ADAM, PART TWO:

the night before, Adam, with the help of his dad, lays out his clothes (including jacket, boots, backpack, etc.). Gordon lets Adam know exactly what is expected of him in the morning and, more importantly, tells Adam, *"I think you have trouble getting ready in the morning because you know that means you are going to child care and will not see Mommy and Daddy all day."*

Wow! Adam not only knows what the rules are regarding dressing, his dad has given him some powerful words to help him make sense of his feelings (and consequently his behavior). At breakfast, Adam is given two healthy choices. If he whines for an inappropriate choice, then breakfast is over. (An easy and obvious way to avoid some of this is to simply not buy food items that you don't want your child eating in the morning.) During the car ride there, Dad begins to tell Adam about his day — working on the computer, making phone calls, etc. He then tells Adam that he will be thinking of him while he is at work and looking forward to seeing him at the end of his day so he can hear all about it. More importantly, he adds, *"You will miss me too but we will see each other at dinner."* This allows Adam to know that the *missing feeling* is OK to have and, in fact, both children and grown-ups experience it. At school, Gordon and Adam have a very specific routine which now includes reading one book and two kisses and one hug. Adam and his teacher then walk to the window where he can wave to his dad as he walks to his car. Adam still wishes Dad didn't have to go to work and Dad still wishes he could spend more time with his son, but both understand what has to be done — and they do it!

For a three and a half-year-old who has never heard this before, there is bound to be some testing before the message gets through.

However, parents who speak to their children about the *missing feeling* from the very start do not often get stuck in a situation that leaves all parties feeling uncertain. In some families the feelings about being apart all day are a little like the elephant in the living room. Everyone knows what is causing tension and hard feelings but no one is willing to talk about it. As in many other situations, parents don't want to give their child the idea about missing them. However, all securely attached children will have strong feelings about being away from their parents — it is a sign of healthy development and we guarantee that no child ever had to be told to miss his or her mom and dad.

Helping your child expect and deal with the feeling of missing her parents reduces uncertainty and can prevent many troubles.

BRIDGING THE GAP

when entering into a child care situation (whether in your own home or a center) allow time to make the *transfer of trust* from parent to caregiver, which is essential for a successful transition. The amount of time it takes will depend on the age of your child, his or her temperament, and the ease with which the triad of parent, child, and caregiver is established. Even an infant, who seems not to notice who is caring for him, needs time to familiarize himself with a new face, new voice, and new touch. A young toddler who is not quite verbal will need time to feel safe in her new environment. An older toddler or preschooler can be helped with homemade books and talking specifically about what will happen.

Work schedules are demanding, but taking the time at the beginning of a new care situation will reap you benefits in the long run. In fact, the investment of time spent here will reap you greater awards than any blue chip stocks.

GUIDELINES FOR ACCLIMATING YOUR
CHILD TO THE CHILD CARE SITUATION

- **visit the school several times before** your child actually starts, at different times of the day if possible.

- **take pictures of his teachers and peers** so you can name them and talk about them at home. These are perfect for your homemade books. If your child is leaving another center, be sure to include pictures of old teachers and friends so they don't seem to just disappear. An older child might even worry that he did something wrong and that is why he is leaving. Make sure you tell your older toddler and preschool-age child the reason for the move (more activities, better location, etc.).

• **schedule the first week so your child** spends a morning, then a morning plus lunch, then a morning plus lunch, plus nap, etc. Lunch and napping away from home are huge transitions for a young child and must be introduced slowly. Mom or Dad are best at helping their child with this process but if necessary, a grandparent or someone else well known to the child can take on the role.

• **allow your child to bring some** transitional objects with him to school. Something he associates with Mom or Dad (an old key ring, a scarf, pictures) all help keep the connection between home and school.

• **call your child if this is allowed** in your school. This will not go on forever:

David's mom began using our child care when he was about three years old. David did great all morning, but at lunch time he fell apart and was so inconsolable that he came to the director's office to calm down. A routine developed: David would call his mother at lunch time and they would speak for a minute or two. This was no easy task as Mom was an occupational therapist who traveled to people's homes and had a different number of appointments each day! Although it was a lot of work on her part, she made sure that we had the number and was willing to interrupt her session so she could speak to her son. After a few weeks, David no longer needed to come into the office or call his mom. In fact, one day, about two months after his last visit to the office, the director saw him in the hall and David said, *"Do you remember when I used to cry in your office? I don't have to do that anymore!"* There was real pride in his voice for this accomplishment, but it could not have been done so effectively if David's mom had not been willing to modify her schedule. Her ability to recognize that her son was missing her and that that was a legitimate feeling made the difference in this little boy's adjustment to child care.

• **if possible, let your child visit your office.** It helps when children have a concrete picture of where you are when you are not together.

THE PARENT'S RELATIONSHIP WITH THE CAREGIVER

hopefully, you are happy with your choice of caregiver and/or center. However, even the best of situations can leave parents sensing the pull between feeling reassured that their child is happy with his caregiver and a bit of sadness that his strong feelings of attachment must be shared with another. Without realizing it, parents can fall into competition with their caregiver. Some parents become "Disneyland parents," ignoring boundaries and expectations that have already been established at school. Many children use the potty perfectly at school only to return home and demand a diaper. Others "forget" how to care for their clothing or clean up, even though these are well-established skills at school.

TIPS FOR A GREAT RELATIONSHIP WITH YOUR CHILD'S CAREGIVER

• **your relationship with the caregiver** is just as important as your child's. Even an infant can perceive tension in the adults around her, so it is essential to establish good communication from the start. If you and the caregiver disagree about major issues, talk it out and find out sooner rather than later if these differences are deal breakers.

• **listen to and respect your caregiver.** We are constantly amazed at the low regard some professional parents have for their caregivers or the centers their children attend. If you have chosen this person/center to nurture your child, you must value their opinions about your child's development and behavior. If you feel you can't, you may be in the wrong situation. No one wants to hear that their child is struggling. When children are in child care, there is a tendency for parents to blame their working for the problem.

Some parents become so anxious that their caregiver notices things about their child that they have not that they put off seeking help for obvious issues:

Ellie was 18 months old when she began child care. She had just begun to walk and still occasionally crawled in the classroom. The teachers were concerned that Ellie did not seem to be able to follow even simple directions and that she had no words, only an incomprehensible babble. They knew that children often concentrate on verbal or motor skills at different times and were concerned that Ellie was delayed in both of these important areas. But age two, Ellie had still not developed words and her play seemed significantly different from the other children in her class. The teachers approached the parents to get a speech evaluation. The parents resisted, citing their doctor's advice to wait until she was three. These teachers were with this child nine to 10 hours a day, five days a week; her doctor saw her every six months or so for a few moments. The parents told the director that the teachers were over-reacting and did not know what was considered "normal" for this age. Eventually, Ellie's delays became so significant that they could not be denied. She ended up attending a class for children with special needs, but earlier intervention might have made a big difference in this little girl's development.

• **inform your caregivers immediately** if there are any significant changes in your child's life. There have been so many times that a child inexplicably begins to act out in class only for the teachers to find out, weeks later, that the child's grandmother died or the father was out of town on business for weeks. Anything that impacts you will impact your child. Keep in mind that on some level even the youngest toddler is aware of changes such as an illness, impending divorce, a move, etc. Sometimes even eagerly anticipated events can bring unwelcome changes in behavior.

It was the end of the week and the end of the school day. Harrison, almost three, always greeted his dad warmly when it was time to go home and easily left school. Today was different. Harrison refused to put on his jacket, repeatedly ran back into the room to see his teachers, and was generally not behaving typically. While Harrison's father was trying to entice him with a trip to the video store, Dad mentioned to the director that he forgot to tell the teachers that Harrison would not be in school all next week because he was going on a trip to see Grandma. The director asked if Harrison knew about the trip and Dad assured the director that he was well-prepared and excited about their plans. The director thought that maybe at Harrison's stage of development he understood about going on the trip but did not fully understand that he was coming back to school. She bent down and said, "Harrison, Dad tells me you are going to visit Grandma. It seems that you are having a hard time saying goodbye to your friends and teachers because you won't be seeing them for a while. But when your trip is over you will come back to school and see...etc." Harrison immediately brightened and began to tell her about the things he would do on his visit. The director called the teachers out of the room and informed them of the trip and they appropriately said their goodbyes and left Harrison with the assurance that they would see him again. Harrison, relaxed and reassured, took his dad's hand and walked out of the building.

Of course, not all problems are so easily solved, but the story illustrates how important it is to make sure that parents share any and all information with the other adults in their child's life.

END-OF-DAY DIFFICULTIES

at the end of a work day, most parents can't wait to see their child. They are anxious to reunite and many parents make the assumption that their child's feelings have kept pace with their own — that he or she is as eager to see them as the parents are to see their child. It comes as a surprise, then, that often parents discover that their child is not quite ready to leave his or her child care, even after a long day:

Michael, three and a half, manages himself during the school day, but as the day draws to a close he anxiously begins to look out the window and seems disheartened when other parents arrive to pick up their children. In fact, Michael's mother is almost always the last parent to pick up, sometimes just making it before the end of the day. Despite Michael's obvious longing to see his mom, the same scene plays out every day at her arrival. Michael just can't seem to disengage from the book he is reading with the teacher or the puzzle he is playing with. He will glance up at Mom and say, "Just another minute. I need to finish this," and continue his activity. Mom stands there awkwardly, wanting to hug her child and hear about his day, but Michael is not interested. Mom will laugh uncomfortably and say, "See how he loves it here. I can't even get him to leave at the end of the day." Although it is possible that he is completely absorbed, it is more likely that Michael is giving Mom a little payback. He needs her to feel the same feelings he has every morning when he is left. Of course, Michael is every bit as anxious as his mom to be with her, but first he needs to let her feelings reflect how he feels — a bit rejected and forsaken. Some parents react to their child's disregard with angry demands; others resort to bribery or cajoling. None of these tactics bring on the desired results. However, if a parent can say, "When it is hard for you to leave and you don't seem to have the time to say hello to me, I think you are mad about being away from me all day. I missed you too and thought about you here in school. I am ready to be together right now and I know that soon you will be ready to be with me and we can go home and have dinner…etc."

The parent who can use words to help her child gain understanding into his behavior will eventually have a child who will begin to recognize why he feels so mad at the end of the day and then be able to move on to behaving appropriately. This takes some time and patience, especially at the beginning, but your words and ability to wait until your child is ready will make all the difference, not just for that day, but for the future as well.

> End-of-Day fights reflect a child's strong feelings about being separated from their parents.

Other children will run appropriately to greet their parent only to pick a fight about some inconsequential thing within moments of their reunion. A dad is surprised and even a bit angry — he does not want to fight now and set an unpleasant tone for the rest of the evening. But try as he might, his child makes a request so unreasonable that the conflict is inevitable. When your child melts down at the end of the day, there are so many things that might be happening. One is simply that, after holding it together and managing school rules for a long day, he lets it all hang out when in the safe haven of his parent's care. Another reason might be just another manifestation of those angry feelings. This child is also saying in the only way he knows how that *"I'm mad that you left me here all day and I need to show you I am angry"* (even if it gets him punished or a treat does not get delivered). These end of the day fights are very common and often conclude with an angry parent carrying a crying child out of the school or giving into one demand after another until the child is placated.

Obviously, these are not effective plans. If Dad can recognize where these feelings are coming from, he can say, *"I see how mad you are. It is hard being away from Dad all day. It is so hard that sometimes you just can't even be happy when you see me even though I am so happy to be here with you. Your words tell me that you are mad that I brought grape juice and not apple juice, but I think you are mad about something more important."* You do not even have to resolve the issue that is causing the tantrum. Just your words, reflecting your child's feelings, will help him gain insight and ultimately control over his behavior. Your child will be so surprised that you understand how he feels and are willing to discuss it that you often see an immediate change in behavior.

SUMMARY

once you have found a caregiver you trust, the key to a successful child care experience is sharing your ideas and feelings, not only with the other adult but with your child as well. Parents who can discuss how hard it is to be apart all day allow their children to freely attach to their caregiver and still happily reunite with them at the end of the day. It is hard for parents, tired from their own day at work, to be patient enough to use their words to reflect back to their child and not resort to threats or bribes. However, if you understand where your child's behavior is stemming from, you can have a plan that will give your child understanding as well as boundaries. Few parents can leave their children without some feelings of doubt or regret, but keep in mind that a caregiver is by a definition just that — a caregiver. And even the most beloved caregiver will never take the place of a loving parent.

Chapter Eight
SIBLING RIVALRY

"We have to divide mother love with our brothers and sisters.
Our parents can help us cope with the loss of our dream
of absolute love. But they cannot make us believe
that we haven't lost it."
— Judith Viorst

the expectation of the birth of a second or subsequent child fills most parents with an excited anticipation that is often tinged with a bit of anxiety. The complete unknown before the birth of a first child is gone; but the worry about the impact a new baby will have on the family unit, most specifically the older sibling(s), is often paramount in parents' minds. The family dynamic will change and that change can challenge the relationship between parent and child. The parent who is not comfortable when his or her child is frustrated or disappointed and who goes to great lengths to avoid conflict may well be surprised by the intensity of the older child's reactions to a new sibling, and may be at a loss for how to help the child handle these new feelings. For, no matter how hard a parent tries, the very existence of a new baby will certainly bring frustration as the needs of that infant will inexorably interfere with the needs of an older child. This fact is inevitable, but there are many things parents can do to ameliorate their older child's feelings and actually use this event (with all of its ambivalent overtones) to help their child develop a positive relationship with his or her new sibling.

even the young-est toddler can sense what their parents are feeling and anticipating, even if they cannot express the concept of a new sibling.

FROM THE BEGINNING:
WHEN TO TELL YOUR OLDER CHILD

**WHEN CHILDREN ARE
24 MONTHS OR LESS APART**
parents often want to know when they should let their child know of

the big event. Some of the timing is dictated by the age of the child. If your children will be very close in age — under 24 months apart — the information will not be understood so much verbally as physically and emotionally. Even the youngest toddlers will be able to sense a mother's changing moods and body as a pregnancy progresses, even if they are unable to firmly grasp the concept of a new baby. Pictures of newborns, pointing out friend's babies, showing them the tiny newborn clothes will all help make the idea of a baby more concrete, but developmentally, your toddler will more concerned about how the pregnancy affects her in the here and now.

As your toddler's awareness increases, you may notice that she is clingier or exhibits sleep disturbances or tantrums. Parents can use these difficult times to talk to their child about the coming event. A young child's receptive language (what they understand) is typically far greater than their expressive language (what they can say) at this age. With this understanding a mom can say to her toddler, *"You get so mad when Mommy is too tired to play (can't pick you up, etc.). Soon the new baby will be here and I will be able to do____ again."* Of course, clinginess, tantrums and the like are typical of this age, with or without a new baby, but do not underestimate your child's ability to perceive the impending changes.

Your sensitivity to your child's moods will be helpful, but sensitivity should not be understood as license. Using words to help your child make sense of her feelings does *not* mean you can allow her to express them inappropriately.

Let's look at a typical scene:

> *Sally is 17 months old and mom is eight months pregnant. Sally tries to climb onto her mother's lap but Mom is uncomfortable and suggests that Sally sit beside her. Sally becomes angry and hits Mom.*

Choices that lay the groundwork to help your child master the feelings she creates offer the best long-term solutions.

Mom has many alternatives: she can ignore the hitting; she can punish Sally with a time out or taking away a toy; she can yell, "Don't hit!" or she can use this conflict to teach a valuable lesson and lay the groundwork for Sally so she can begin to learn how to master difficult and frustrating situations. The first three alternatives may result in a temporary "win" for Mom but will not prevent the same type of interaction happening in the future. So what's a mother to do?

LET'S TAKE ANOTHER LOOK:

• **sally hits mom.** Mom makes a reasonable assumption that Sally is mad that she can't get what she wants (Mom's lap) and does not have the verbal skills to adequately express her feelings.

• **mom says,** *"Sally, when you hit me I know you are very mad — you want to sit on my lap and you can't because of the baby inside."* Just the identification of the feeling should get Sally to listen.

• **mom continues,** *"I know there are lots of times you get mad because you and I can't do what we used to do. It's OK to be mad but you* **cannot** *hit Mommy."*

• **"we need to figure out** *another way for you to tell me you are mad."* At this juncture, Mom can give suggestions (an older, verbal child can think of her own). Hitting a pillow or stomping a foot and saying "mad" work quite well for the young toddler.

• **if sally persists** in hitting Mom, Mom does a modified inverted time out (as described in the Discipline chapter) by standing up and turning away from Sally. (For a child this young, it is not safe for you to leave the room.)

• **as she turns, mom says,** *"If you hit I will not sit next to you. I want to play with you but not if you hit."* It may take a few tries, but what Sally really wants is Mom and she will soon learn that to have her she cannot hit.

Some parents feel that there should be some punishment involved and that this is not a strong enough reaction. But again, the ultimate goal of discipline is teaching, not shaming. If you can teach your child a rule about relating to you and his or her siblings, that is a very successful day.

let's say you place your child in time out. You will have to pick her up or lead her to a time out place and more than likely have to remind her to stay still until the time out is over. Your young toddler does not see this in the same way you do; in fact, in most time out situations there is so much interaction between parent and child that it becomes a powerful reinforcer for the negative behavior. Even if you are mad, you are still giving attention to your child and children will most certainly work very hard to keep your attention — even if it is negative! It takes more time to identify feelings and think of alternatives, but teaching an important lesson that can be used again and again should take longer than a stop gap measure.

WHEN THE AGE GAP IS 24 MONTHS OR MORE

many books and pediatricians advise not telling a child until two or three months before the event because small children do not have a firm sense of time. While this may be true, it is also true that your child's other senses are very well developed. Every typically developing child will perceive changes in his or her mother's mood and body, understand on some level the adult conversations about the "baby," and notice differences in the house as parents prepare for the birth. Our rule of thumb is simple: once the news is public you must inform your child. For the younger child, a simple statement that he or she is going to become a big sister or brother when it is warm out or at the nearest holiday time is a good start. Parents should add that the baby is growing inside Mommy's body in a special place called a womb or a uterus. We would avoid causing the common confusion when you call your womb or uterus a tummy. Children in this age group are well aware that food goes in tummies and that everybody has tummies — both boys and girls. Yet, only females carry a baby in their bodies. Children also realize that their tummies sometimes hurt before a bowel movement and if your older child is going through potty training, this can lead to even further confusion about how the baby got in there and how it is going to get out. If the concept of a uterus or womb is new, this can also be an opportunity to introduce this part of normal bodies to your child. You can certainly say that it looks like the baby is growing in a tummy but that is because the special baby place is right next to the tummy.

Once you are ready to make news of your pregnancy more public, it is also time to be sure your child(ren) knows.

so why go to so much trouble to inform your child properly and so early? Because young children most often develop challenging behavior in response to a new sibling when parents do not share this special news appropriately.

THESE TWO EXAMPLES MAY HELP TO ILLUSTRATE THIS POINT.

- *Cathy was a four-year-old, with one older and one younger sister. She was doing well in her pre-K class when suddenly she refused to enter the classroom when her mom brought her to school. Cathy would literally dig in her heels at the doorway, wail, scream, and absolutely exhaust herself and the adults with her behavior. This was such atypical behavior for this well developed girl that after some probing questions with Mom the situation became more clear. Cathy's mom had recently discovered she was pregnant for a fourth time, just six months after the birth of her third child.*

This mom was very ambivalent about this pregnancy. Because of her mixed feelings, she did not tell Cathy or her older sister but was discussing her ambivalence with her husband, mother, and friends. Although she never directly told Cathy, this bright, perceptive preschooler overheard bits and pieces of the adult conversations and made her own faulty conclusions resulting in her confusing and extreme reaction to leaving her mother at preschool. By the time the situation had developed, Cathy's mom had already come to accept and even look forward to this new addition but still had not officially told her older children. After consultation, Mom shared the news with her other children and Cathy's unusual behavior literally stopped the next day. This mom did not connect the overheard conversations with Cathy's behavior but, in fact, children typically react in a negative fashion when they are not appropriately brought into the information loop.

- **michael's mother went to see** *her preschool director about a change in her two and a half-year-old's behavior. Michael was clinging to his mother's side while she described his tantrums and generally difficult behavior. The director suggested that they talk about these issues when Michael was not present. Mom agreed, but persisted with questions about moving Michael out of his bed, switching rooms, and the like. The director, sensitive to Michael's feelings about the conversation, asked him what he thought about the new baby. The director was quite surprised when the mom answered for him, "Oh, he doesn't know about the baby yet. Our doctor told us not to tell him until a couple of weeks before the birth."*

Parents often do not appreciate just how much their toddler and preschooler can understand. Michael's mother **had** told him about the baby — with every conversation he overheard in the grocery store, on the phone, and with family and friends. This unclear communication can lead a child to come to some pretty confusing and disturbing conclusions and can have a surprising and negative impact on your child's behavior.

once you have told your older child about the baby, you can expect a range of reactions. Some children seem thrilled by the prospect; others will voice disappointment. Don't be fooled by either response, no matter how extreme. There is no way for a preschool-age or younger child to truly anticipate what it will be like to have a baby in the house. Respond to all questions and statements as truthfully as possible. To the excited child, you might say, *"I am so glad you can't wait to see the baby — it will be fun — but there may also be some things you may not like."* To the child who is already planning fratricide, you may say something like, *"I hear that you have some worries about what it will be like once the baby is here. That's OK.*

In discussing the new baby, it is important to know that your goal is to respond honestly to your child's feelings. The goal is not to try to change your child's feelings.

I felt the same when Grandma was going to have Uncle Bobby (or any relationship that is known to your child and makes sense). Once the baby is born you can always let me know with your words if you are upset or unhappy. Mommy and Daddy will listen and together we will make a plan for you." Notice that this discussion does not talk about how wonderful it is to have a new brother or sister, or what good friends they will be. You are simply responding honestly to your child's feelings but not trying to convince him to feel otherwise. If you do, you may experience great frustration and, in that frustration, leave your child with the sense that he has not pleased you by having the *correct* feeling.

Other questions that older preschoolers ask are, *"How did the baby get started?"* and *"How will it get out?"* Be prepared for these questions and, again, honest answers that do not give more information than the child can handle are the most appropriate.

NEXT STEPS

your child has the basic information but the baby's birth is now impending. There are many things you can do to prepare your child for the birth which can lessen but, of course, not completely eliminate future conflicts.

• **make a book**. Although you can buy books about the new baby, a homemade book, just about your family, is one of the most invaluable tools a parent can prepare. We suggest using an old photo album, the kind with the acetate pages. You can name the book something like "Danny Becomes a Big Brother." This book can start with pictures of Mom when she was expecting Danny and pictures of him as an infant. Accompanying words will describe how he ate, where he slept, who took care of him, and include pictures of close family members and caregivers. Add pictures of Mom pregnant now and include pictures of Danny's likely caregivers when you go into the hospital. Add pictures of Danny doing his daily routine when you are not with him. Your absence will be the most difficult part of the first few days (at least for him!) and your sensitivity at this time will help him through this short but fundamental separation.

• **change sleeping arrangements well in advance of the birth.** If your child is under three and loves his crib, you might want to consider borrowing another crib for the newborn until a more natural time occurs for your oldest to make this transition. If, however, you feel the time is right for the change, make it at least two months before the baby is due. In fact, if possible, it is helpful for you to take down the crib (with your child's help and attention, of course!) and store it for a few weeks before putting it up again for the new baby. An older child will not be fooled by this; it is simply a way to help him let go.

• **attend your hospital's sibling classes.** These classes will help give your child a concrete image of where you will be. If allowed, arrange to have your older child visit you and the baby in the hospital. If this cannot occur, make sure you call him and reassure him that you are all right and will be home soon to take care of him.

A word about children attending the actual birth. Despite the availability of this practice in some birthing centers, we strongly suggest that children not be present at a birth. A child under five or six can in no way under-

stand the discomfort of labor, his or her mother's changed moods, or the blood that accompanies even an easy birth. An older school-age child (over 12) may be able to manage it, but remember, a three or four-year-old who says "yes" when asked if he or she wishes to be there has absolutely no basis for his or her answer. This is an adult event.

● **don't make too many changes right before the birth.** Some changes are unavoidable but, if possible, put off moving to a new house or starting a new preschool in the weeks before the birth. Many parents ask me about beginning potty training. If you have a child who is close to three, you may want to start the process even if you are seven or eight months pregnant. On the other hand, if your older one is just two you may be wise to wait until the baby is well established in the household.

● **make grandma mad.** Although it may seem to fly in the face of logic, if you go into labor in the middle of the night, wake up your child to say goodbye. Nothing is more frightening to young children than to awaken to find Mom and Dad gone — even if their beloved grandma is there. So although your mother or other caregiver may curse you, wake up your little one with the assurance that you will see (or talk) to him tomorrow after the baby is born.

WHEN BABY COMES HOME

the big day has finally come. You are bringing home the new addition with high expectations for your new family unit. A new baby brings a special exhilaration but it also brings exhaustion, physical discomfort, and short fuses. Even the most patient parent can become overwhelmed and anxious by the demands of more than one child. This anxiety can lead to difficulty in accepting an older child's ambivalence about his sibling because his feelings seem to reflect your own apprehension! To convince your older child (and yourself!) that everything is going to be fine, parents often fall into the trap of telling their child that, *"You love your baby sister."* In fact, Danny feels quite unsure just how he feels and with no one confirming that it is OK to have conflicting feelings about his new role, Danny may begin to use inappropriate behaviors to let his parents know that something is not right. If you can accept that your older child is going to have ambiva-

> Even the most patient parent can become overwhelmed and anxious by the demands of more than one child.

lent feelings about this new baby and, in fact, use the inevitable conflicts as a teaching tool, you will be well on your way to a more peaceful family unit. Although you cannot avoid the inevitable, there are some things you can do and say to help your older child adjust to his new role and position in the family.

• **have a plan.** Parents who anticipate when their older child may have the most difficulty are ahead of the game. One of the times that almost always stirs up big feelings in the older sibling is feeding time. Whether you breast or bottle feed, you will probably want this to be a special, quiet time for you and your newborn. Your older child will look at this time as a complete usurpation of what used to be *hers* and will often pick the moment you sit down to need a drink, some food, a toy, or anything else that will take your attention away from the baby.

You can help this situation by preparing a *Big Brother/Big Sister Bag* for your oldest even before you have the baby. This can be any sort of canvas or sturdy bag that you will fill with items that can be independently used by your child. Some examples are any toy that is not messy (this is not the time for Play-doh) such as a magnetic art board or a simple puzzle; a juice box; and a little container with dried cereal or other "neat" food.

As you are about to sit down, say to your child, *"Danny, it is time for me to feed the baby. Here is your special bag. Let's see what is in there today."* Danny may still whine and tell you he wants apple juice, not orange juice, but now you can calmly reply, *"I think it is hard for you to see me feed the baby when you want me to play with you. You can use the things in your special bag and when I am through we can…"* Danny may sit quietly or he may continue to badger you but if he does, your job is not to cajole, negotiate, or bribe. You can feel content knowing that you DID meet your older child's needs the best you could under the circumstances and continue to feed the baby, hopefully enjoying that special time together. Your consistent responses will help Danny see that you are, in fact, thinking of him as well as the baby, and he will eventually learn that he will get his turn.

• **understand overlapping needs.** The closer in age your children are, the more their needs will overlap. An 18-month-old is, in essence, still an infant because she still depends on her parent for the majority of her physical needs. Her sense of delayed gratification (ability to wait to get her needs met) is short and her verbal skills are limited, so it is more likely that she will use physical means to get your attention. On the other hand, a child of four can usually dress herself, get a simple snack, and toilet herself without adult assistance. She may not be happy about it, but she can understand what it means to *"wait a minute."*

An older preschooler has also begun to develop interests outside of the home. She will want to spend time away from her parents, at a friend's house or at school. To an 18–month-old, however, her parent is still the center of the universe. It is not easy, but try to balance meeting the needs of both your newborn and your young toddler.

When you cannot meet the needs of your toddler as immediately as you would like, you can say, *"It is hard to wait. You look mad. I will help you soon."* What you don't want to do is feel so guilty that you apologize to your child or allow her to hurt you or the baby. It may be hard for a young toddler to be displaced, but you can let your child know that although you understand the feeling, you will not tolerate negative behavior.

● **expect some regression.** Many preschoolers who have long ago given up the pacifier or bottle or their crib will want to try it out again once the new baby is born. They may even ask to nurse again. We do not suggest allowing an older child to nurse again; the message is too confusing (*"You are a big boy, but sure, nurse like a baby."*). You can simply say, *"This is how you were fed when you were a baby; now you drink from a cup, etc."*

If you find your preschooler lying on the floor sucking one of his little sister's pacifiers, reflect back to him that he is *"pretending to be a baby and that a pacifier helps babies who cannot talk feel better."* Remind him that he has big boy words that he can use to tell Mom and Dad about his feelings.

Another common scenario is when the older child suddenly becomes extremely possessive about a baby item or toy that he has long outgrown. If this happens frequently, you can ask your older one to pick out one or two things that are so special to him that he can put away and not give to the baby. Then you must stick to the rule.

If he continues to whine and become upset that the baby is *"using his stuff,"* remind him that he chose what the baby cannot use. End of discussion. Case closed. Do not let him get to you so that you end up buying something extra for Danny to quell your feelings of guilt about giving him a baby sister.

• **be suspicious of the child who shows no jealousy.** Virtually every typically developing child will have some negative feelings about their younger sibling. When a parent tells us that the older one is "perfect with the baby," we have our doubts.

A story about three-year-old Rose may help illustrate:

> *Rose's mother told her doctor that she absolutely loves the baby and there is no problem there. However, Rose has begun to get pretty mad at her parents and has begun hitting them both. "Well, at least she is not hitting the baby," Rose's mom laughed. In truth, this is no laughing matter. Rose's mother must stop that behavior immediately, but she must also help Rose gain some insight into why she wants to hurt her parents. Rose's mom can say to her, "You may not hit me — I know you are angry about all the time the baby takes, but you can use your words (or draw a mad picture, etc.) to tell me. You cannot hit me." Does Rose really want to hurt her mother? No, what she wants is her mom's full attention. Then how do you teach Rose a more appropriate way to get what she wants? It is to take away what Rose wants most — her mom. If Rose persists in hitting, Rose's mom can pick up the baby, walk into her bedroom, and have an inverted time out (see chapter on Discipline for a complete description). This will let Rose know that although her feeling is legitimate, her actions are not acceptable. (This action can only be taken once the older child is old enough to be safely left in a room on her own.)*

• **be wary of the sibling "hug,"**

The following story is absolutely classic:

> *Corey is 30 months old and has a six-week-old brother, Adam. Mom asks if there is anything she can do to help Corey understand how to be gentler with the baby. Mom says, "Corey simply loves the baby but whenever she goes to hug him, she ends up hugging too hard and the baby cries. I know she doesn't mean to hurt him." Of course she does! This is the perfect description of an older sibling's ambivalent feelings. On one hand, Corey does have some positive feelings about her brother, but these positive feelings are in constant conflict with the not-so-loving feelings that co-exist within her. Mom can say,*

"Corey, I see that that hug turned into a squeeze that made Adam cry. I know that you have two very big feelings inside of you — one is a hugging feeling; the other is a squeezing feeling! When you feel the squeezing feeling you will have to figure out another way to tell me you are mad (or sad)."Depending on the verbal skills of the child, you can make a plan of action. If Corey persists in hurting the baby, the use of the inverted time out can be used. Remember, when Corey does choose a more positive action, praise her by describing what you saw: "It looks like you were thinking of squeezing Adam but instead you used your words. You followed your plan!" Steer clear of calling her a "good girl" because the inevitable question in her mind with that type of praise is that, when she is unable to follow her plan, is she a "bad girl"?

This method is effective with children as young as 24 months.

● **use parallel stories.** A parallel story is a nifty way to let your child know that you understand her feelings without talking directly about her. For instance, if Corey is still struggling with the feelings that make her want to hurt her brother, her parent could use a story about another little girl who loved her baby brother but still sometimes really wished that he would go back to the hospital. Parents will often ask if this type of story is not *"putting ideas into their child's head."* Without doubt, your child has developed a slew of negative and confusing ideas all on her own. What these stories can do is to help her begin to gain some understanding, which can then lead to better choices. Parents can use real children who are known to their child, stories about their childhood if they apply, or simply make up a scenario to match the situation. It is really a case of "the story is the same, but the names have been changed to protect the innocent." Tell these stories at a quiet time, such as after a bath or when riding in the car. Most children love these stories, especially if you can use yourself as the child in the example.

Occasionally, a child will actually cover her ears and say she *"won't listen."* Bingo! If this occurs, you know you have hit the hot button exactly. Persist, but perhaps change the story slightly so your child can begin to hear it.

● **child care and preschool.** Many children will have some difficulty separating from their parents after a sibling's birth. The thought of that new baby getting Mom and/or Dad all to himself can make it difficult to go to school alone — even if school is a favorite place. Think of going to preschool as your child's job; you can be sympathetic but firm about his attendance. Use parallel stories or talk about his feelings at a time other than right before you are trying to get him in the car. You can tell him that you understand it is hard to go when you are home with the baby, but he needs to go to school. Your firmness and lack of ambivalence in your voice and stance will give him the right message.

Most preschool directors and teachers are aware of this regression and should help you with a plan if your child really seems to get stuck. Many moms who work full time outside of the home keep their older child in care for the same hours and days as before the birth. Although it certainly makes sense to keep the older child's routine as normal as possible and it is essential to *hold the spot* for your child in school, we recommend a modification of the schedule if possible. Parents want their limited time at home to just be with the baby so they send the older ones to child care for their full hours. However, your child will know that you are home with the baby and leaving her at school. This makes the initial displacement seem even harder to bear. Think about sending your child for mornings only or least significantly shortening her day. It is certainly easier for the parent to leave the older one at school and avoid having to deal with more than one child at home. However, it is precisely those moments that will naturally occur in the course of a day which give you and your child the opportunity to figure out how to handle the rollercoaster emotions that follow the birth of a new baby.

• **can all inappropriate behavior be blamed on the baby?** Not all, but many behaviors which do not seem directly linked to the baby can actually be the result of becoming a big sibling. Sleep issues, new fears, destructive behavior, and school problems can all be related. If your child is not showing any physical or verbal aggression toward the new baby or you, but begins to exhibit other troubling behaviors, a little detective work can usually pinpoint the underlying cause.

An example might help:

> Paul, age three and a half, has been terrific with his new baby brother, his father reports. However, in preschool and at home he has begun to become unusually destructive — for instance, knocking down a friend's block tower and even destroying a favorite toy of his own. Paul's dad recognizes that there is some significant anger

behind these actions. *Where did the anger come from?* Dad knows that, except for the new baby, everything else in the house has been status quo (no big separations, illness, etc.). Quite logically Dad believes that maybe the baby is causing the anger. However, Paul seems to love the baby — never hurting him, running to get a diaper, and showing him off to friends and family. Despite this, Dad plunges in after Paul wrecks one of his own creations and says, "Paul, when I see a boy throwing his toy so hard that it breaks, I think he must be **very** angry. I think you may be pretty angry at Mom and Dad and the new baby. I know I would feel that way (great time for a parallel story) and it is OK to feel angry. You can tell me how you feel and I won't get mad." Paul may even deny that he is mad, but he has heard an important statement from his dad and received an even more important gift — knowing that the most important person in his world understands how he feels. Now, even though Dad understands, he must still follow through on the logical consequences of Paul's actions. Feelings are always accepted but inappropriate behavior is not.

ISN'T THERE AN EASIER WAY?

for most parents, learning to speak to their children in the ways described above is harder than learning a foreign language. In fact, it is harder. Very few of us come to parenting with any specific skills, and yet we soon learn that we need to develop some new ways of thinking and reacting to deal with the inevitable conflicts and frustrations that occur when raising a family. Many parenting books offer simple rules for disciplining children and *stopping* sibling rivalry. These books become popular because all parents would love a *magic bullet* that they can use to help them parent more effectively. In fact, some of these techniques can lead to short term success, but will ultimately fail because they do not include the child as a partner in the process. There is little opportunity for the child to generalize what he has learned from one situation and apply it to a similar one in the

There are quick paths to quick peace after a family expands, but we recommend the longer-term value of seeking an approach that firmly promotes the child as a partner in his/her own adaptations to change.

future because he has not been given the tools to master his own behavior.

Although our culture has changed dramatically in the past decades, the basics of parenting have not: it is still messy, inconvenient, and time consuming! The relationships between siblings will likely be the longest, most enduring ones they have. It takes a lot of time and effort, but these techniques can be critical to establishing healthy family interactions from the very beginning.

W

Chapter Nine

IN SUMMARY

"A family in harmony
will prosper
in everything."

— Chinese Proverb

for many parents, conflict with their children is seen as failure on their part. They take full responsibility for keeping their children happy and content and see resistance to rules as a breakdown in the parent/child relationship. We have presented a different paradigm for thinking about the most common conflicts that naturally occur between parent and child. Instead of seeing conflict as a barrier to the needs to love and be loved, we demonstrate how conflict is not only natural but *helpful* in creating a peaceful family. That conflict enhances a child's confidence and competence as they figure out solutions to their own problems.

Our hope is that you were able to mine two major nuggets of value from reading this book. The first is a shift in the way you think about conflict; the second is the acquisition of specific approaches to resolve conflicts.

THE APPROACH TO CONFLICT

we have tried to present a compelling case for embracing rather than shunning the conflict that occurs when your child desires her own way rather than follow family rules. Differences of desire and preference are present between any two people, so it makes only sense that such differences will be present between every child and parent. The most common examples conflict-producing differences concern the issues of sleep, feeding, discipline, toilet training, sibling rivalry, and child care. In each instance, we have found that parents often

> Parents often choose approaches that avoid dealing with their child when they exhibit a behavior that does not match the parents' desire.

choose approaches that avoid dealing with their child when they exhibit a behavior that does not match the parents' desire. These approaches are designed to produce peace instead of conflict and follow two main paths: an over reliance on nurturance or an over reliance on authority. Both nurturing and authority are natural, vital, and necessary elements of parenting, but using either as a sole solution often leads to problems.

> Both nurturing and authority are natural, vital, and necessary elements of parenting, but using either as a sole solution often leads to problems.

in the case of avoiding conflict through nurturing, parents frequently experience conflict as a possible catastrophe, an opening of a chasm or abyss. Conflicts lead to protests from our young children, and these protests are experienced as possible moments of trauma. If the parent's goal is to provide the most loving and secure environment, then a disagreement could be seen as a threat to that very basic goal.

in the case of avoiding conflict through an over reliance on authority, conflict is also experienced as a possible catastrophe, in this case the possible destruction of the authority of the parent. If the parent's goal is to create a home respectful of rules, then a disagreement can still be seen a threat to that very basic goal.

both approaches contain the same misunderstanding and, interestingly, miss the same insight: that young children *need* conflict. They need conflict to help them really learn what is important, how to negotiate for what they want, and how to relate to people who have different wants than they do. Children seek conflict as the place where answers to important questions reside. Conflict does not threaten family love or rules, it defines both. We describe a perspective in which the child's challenges and the conflicts they create give parents an opportunity to both demonstrate their love *and* their authority. In essence, with an effective set of responses to the most common sources of conflict, parents deepen their love and strengthen their authority.

> With an effective set of responses to the most common sources of conflict, parents deepen their love and strengthen their authority.

FROM PERSPECTIVE TO PRACTICE

perspective on struggle is important but parents must also have the tools to employ very specific approaches to managing each of the most common sources of conflict between child and parent. Without these tools the parent may have some idea of what to do but lack the confidence to interact with their child in a calm, consistent and thoughtful manner.

The very specific guidance we have offered is the product of many years of working with families in pre-school and pediatric practice settings. This guidance is distilled from the wisdom of many, many parents and their children; from listening rather than directing; from observing what actually works and what does not. We have offered this advice to many families over many years and found that these ideas worked in nearly every instance.

Who's the Boss: Moving Families from Conflict to Collaboration offers field-tested and proven advice containing very specific step-by-step guidance on just how to manage the following challenges of parenthood:

- Helping your infant **sleep** all night so that you can get a night's sleep.

- Resolving conflicts around **feeding** so that meals can be peaceful.

- Providing meaningful and effective **discipline** so that your child is safe and your home calmer.

- Discussing specific, **special discipline** situations that challenge even the most adept parent.

- Helping your toddler decisively conclude the toilet training process with **toilet mastery**.

- Addressing how to **manage child care** so that flare ups are infrequent and the whole experience can be enjoyed by child and parent.

- Guiding young **siblings to manage their rivalries** so that parents and children can live together more effectively.

our wish is that *Who's the Boss: Moving Families from Conflicts to Collaboration* will help you understand and accept your child's need to engage in conflict; that you will incorporate the specific guidance techniques we have outlined on these pages; and that this book will provide you with valuable steps towards satisfying, joyful parenting.

W

Reading List

Dixon, Suzanne and Stein, Martin. *Encounters with Children: Pediatric Behavior and Development.* Mosby, 2005.

Mogal, Wendy. *The Blessings of a Skinned Knee.* New York, NY: Penguin, 2001.

Weisberger, Eleanor. *Your Young Child and You.* New York, NY: Dutton Adult, 1979.

Weisberger, Eleanor. *When Your Child Needs You.* Bethesda, MD: Adler and Adler Publishers, 1987.

Winnicott, D.W. *Babies and their Mothers.* London: Free Association Books, 1987; Reading, MA: Addison-Wesley Publishing. Perseus Press, 1990.

Index

Authors

SUSAN GLASER, MA

susan b. glaser m.a. is an educational psychologist who has worked in private practice with parents of young children, and is also an early childhood educator. She was the Director of Early Childhood Services for the Jewish Community Center of Cleveland for 15 years and currently works as a national consultant in that field. She has had more than 30 years of experience presenting workshops for parents that support young families as they deal with the common developmental issues of childhood.

Ms. Glaser wrote a monthly article on parenting for a local Cleveland publication and has had articles published in newspapers and national early childhood publications. She is married and the mother of three grown children.

W

ARTHUR LAVIN, MD

arthur lavin, md, is a pediatrician with more than 20 years of experience in private practice. Dr. Lavin, trained at Harvard, Ohio State University, and MIT, is a board certified subspecialist in newborn medicine. He has served on a number of national committees of the American Academy of Pediatrics.

Dr. Lavin has received international recognition from Microsoft and GE for being one of the pioneers in the use of technology in the practice of medicine. He is married and has three children.

W

ABOUT THIS BOOK

body text is set in Galápagos Design Group's Kennedy ® GD and the bold accent type in ITC Franklin Gothic Heavy. Illustrations copyright ©1996 by Havana Street, fee paid.

Galápagos Design Group provides high quality type products to the graphics arts, printing, and publishing industries. In addition, GDG clients include many major type foundries.

ITC (International Typeface Corporation) is well known for classic design fonts such as Franklin Gothic. Based on Morris Fuller Benton's original Roman face of 1902, the current sans serif was created in the 1950s as a response to the world-wide popularity of Helvetica. The format used here was developed for ITC by Font Haus of Boston, the fourth largest font digital font resource in the world.

Havana Street is E.J. Garces and Emery Wang. They have been creating 1940s-style illustrations for the royalty-free market since 1996.

W